ACTION AMIGA

Computer Graphics Animation and Video Production Manual

John Warren Oakes

T0130814

UNIVERSITY
PRESS OF
AMERICA

Lanham • New York • London

Copyright © 1989 by

University Press of America,® Inc.

4720 Boston Way
Lanham, MD 20706

3 Henrietta Street
London WC2E 8LU England

British Cataloging in Publication Information Available

Library of Congress Cataloging-in-Publication

Oakes, John Warren.
Action Amiga.
Includes index.
1. Amiga (Computer)—Programming. 2. Computer
graphics. 3. Video recordings—Production and
direction. I. Title.
QA76.8.A177025   1988   006.6'765   88–26158
ISBN 0–8191–7209–X (pbk. : alk. paper)

Acknowledgments

Amiga, Commodore, Kickstart, Workbench, Extras, Transformer, GraphiCraft, Genlock and Sidecar are trademarks of Commodore Business Machines.

DeluxePaint and DeluxePaint II, Deluxe Video, Deluxe Music Construction Set, Instant Music are trademarks of Electronic Arts.

Aegis Images and Aegis Animator are trademarks of Aegis.

Digi-View and Digi-Paint are trademarks of New Tek.

Okimate 20 is a trademark of Okidata.

Cibachrome is a trademark of Ilford.

Ektachrome 200, Tri-X, and Super XX are trademarks of Eastman Kodak.

Xerox 6500 is a trademark of Xerox.

BFK is a trademark of Rives Paper.

Arches is a trademark of Arches Paper.

Kwik-Print is distributed solely by Light Impressions.

DEDICATION

This book is dedicated to my students.

Table of Contents

Introduction

During 1985, Commodore Business Machines introduced the Amiga personal computer. It presently is the best personal computer for artists selling for less than a thousand dollars . The Amiga's graphic capabilities are appropriate for the creation of images by freehand drawing and coloring, animation, desktop publishing and video. Selections are made from 4,096 color variations of hue, saturation and value. In high resolution mode it displays 640 pixels across the screen and 400 pixels from top to bottom on a red, green and blue monitor which combines these light primaries to form the colors on the screen. A pixel is the smallest dot or point on the screen. A line of pixel points in high resolution is close to the thinness of a pencil line drawn on paper. This high resolution and expanded palette coupled with 512k or more of memory with the addition of external memory boards presents artists and designers with an affordable and powerful system capable of creating computer graphics and electronic art.

Many excellent software programs have been designed for the Amiga which are compatable with each other sharing the IFF format. They may be used to create art by computer without prior computer experience or any knowledge of programming. This manual will introduce some of these programs and present applications for their use. In addition, various hardware peripherals are described which allow multi-media and video production. There are few illustrations in this book. The book should be used with the various programs operating as their own illustrations on the monitor screen.

The last chapter is a gallery of computer generated images. However, no print can equal the light transmission of the screen with its 4096 colors.

Art in the past was refreshed by the introduction of new colors, the oil medium, paint in tubes, printing processes like etching, lithography and serigraphy, the acrylic medium, photography and video. The computer is a new tool offering unique applications for artists and designers. I hope this book will assist you and encourage you in your explorations into the possibilities of this contemporary medium.

CHAPTER ONE

USING THE AMIGA PERSONAL COMPUTER

The Commodore Amiga computer consists of the following equipment called hardware. The computer itself is about the size of a small stereo. This unit is called the central processing unit and it processes information entered into the computer by the KEYBOARD or by the MOUSE CONTROL through software programs. Presently, there are three models available, the A500, A1000 and the A2000. The KEYBOARD looks like a small typewriter with a few extra keys and a calculator keypad on the right side. The return key is pressed to ENTER lines of code in programming or commands when using the DISK operating system. The Amiga uses AmigaDOS for its DISK operating system and commands are entered in through the CLI or Command Line Interpreter. The MOUSE CONTROL fits under the palm of your hand and has two buttons. The left mouse button is called the SELECT button and the right mouse button is called the MENU button. The cord and the buttons should be pointing toward the MONITOR screen. By moving the mouse you can position a cursor or a marker on the MONITOR screen which, when placed over commands in a MENU BAR, allows you to select different items from the MENU. Do this by pulling the MENU names down into view, pressing down the right button to highlight your selections, then, release the right mouse button. Select from windows by clicking with the left button on control boxes. This is the usual procedure for programs that use the MENU and MOUSE for control. Ordinarily, it is a quick way to give commands to the computer and is faster than entering typewritten lines of code. Some programs combine both mouse and KEYBOARD command lines or FUNCTION KEYS for expanded operations. The MONITOR screen shows the output of the computer program and is like a television screen but has higher resolution. This is the essential hardware for operating the computer.

All the electronic components: the central processing unit, the monitor and a printer (if you have one) should be plugged into a multiple outlet strip which has a surge suppressor on it and an off-on switch. This strip is plugged into the wall outlet for electricity with its switch in the off position. The off-on rocker switch for the central processing unit is on the left side of the A1000. It should be in the on position. The switch for the MONITOR is on the front of the MONITOR on the right just below the screen.

1

Push in the panel switch to turn on the MONITOR. The printer switch may be turned on when you are ready to begin printing. The switch on the MONITOR and the computer central processing unit may be left in the on position using the off-on switch of the multiple outlet switch when you want to turn on and turn off the entire configuration. This will save wear and costly replacement of the other switches. Never unplug the computer central processing unit while it is operating. If this unit is turned off or becomes unplugged by accident, never turn it back on without waiting ten seconds. The system should not be used during electrical storms. When you wish to power down or turn off the system, simply turn off the switch on the power strip. The next time you turn on the system, just turn on the power strip and the system should be on. A red light will appear on the central processing unit front panel at the lower left and on the lower right of the MONITOR. If these lights do not come on when you turn on the power strip, turn their switches on. The central processing unit is always turned on first, then any peripherals like monitors and printers.

The hardware system should be protected from extremes of heat or cold. Do not block the ventilation slots on the backs of the units. Positively no liquids nor food should be in the same room with computers. Liquids will damage the KEYBOARD and computer and food crumbs can make the keys on the KEYBOARD malfunction and stick. Excessive humidity will corrode the heads that read the disks and other components of the electrical system. Smoke is very damaging to disks and the heads that read the disks. Do not smoke in the same room with the computer. Disks that have been warped by heat or cold or which have been subjected to moisture should not be used in the computer. Adhering to these precautions will help insure the efficient operation of the system. The Amiga uses 3 and 1/2 inch double sided, double density microdisks in the disk drive built into the central processing unit or in extra external disk drives. The magnetic DISK is encased in a plastic protective cover which does not come off. Handle the microdisk by this cover. Do not explore the DISK surface with fingers or anything else. The DISK is inserted in a horizontal slot recessed into the right side of the front panel of the A1000 and A2000 central processing units. It is on the right side of the A500. The right corner of the DISK is cut at a 45 degree angle and an arrow is molded into the upper left of the plastic to indicate the side and edge to place in the slot. A small switch on the opposite

2

end and opposite side of the DISK controls whether the DISK can be written to and store information or if it is to be read only and not allowed to store information. This switch may be moved with a fingernail or with care by using a pen point to slide the plastic button. When this button is in the outside notch the DISK is protected and the button must be moved to the inside notch to store information. Additional DISK drives for 3 and 1/2 inch disks are available which may be placed next to the central processing unit. A 5 and 1/4 inch drive is needed to use disks of this size with a Transformer or Sidekick system which allows the Amiga to run MS-DOS programs.

To remove a DISK, press the eject button under the DISK slot on the lower right side of the central processing unit or the DISK drive. Never remove a DISK when the drive is on and a red light is visible on the panel near the eject button. This will damage the DISK and make it unreadable. Always wait about 15 seconds after the light goes out to be sure the drive is off. Sometimes the light will go off momentarily and come back on as the DISK head continues to read the DISK. Be patient and don't risk losing all your work.

It is good insurance to make back-up disks of all your work in case you do damage a DISK or if some dust gets on the DISK. Eventually disks wear to the point where the head cannot read them so you will need back-ups in any case.

This introduces you to the Amiga personal computer. Additional information is available in the operating manual and an excellent tutorial program is on the Amiga Extras DISK. To run the Amiga Tutor program turn on the computer as described above. When the screen lights up, a symbol of the KICKSTART DISK will appear. Insert the KICKSTART 1.1 DISK when this happens. Next, the icon for the WORKBENCH DISK will come on screen. Remove the KICKSTART DISK and insert the WORKBENCH 1.1 DISK. When this DISK is through loading and the drive light is out, remove the WORKBENCH DISK and Insert the Amiga Extras DISK. The MONITOR screen will DISPLAY two icons, one for WORKBENCH and one for Amiga Extras. Position the red arrow marker on the Amiga Extras icon and press the left mouse button quickly two times. This will open the window and DISPLAY an icon for the Amiga Tutor. Position the mouse arrow marker on this icon and double-click with the left mouse button to LOAD the Amiga Tutor program. Follow the directions of this

3

animated tutorial. After completing this instruction
you will be ready to experience the exciting graphic
programs described in the next chapters.

CHAPTER TWO

USING DELUXEPAINT

One of the most popular software programs for computer graphics is DELUXEPAINT created by Dan Silva for Electronic Arts. It is a freehand drawing program that simulates drawing and painting on the MONITOR screen.

This first chapter will include a great deal of detailed, step-by-step instruction operating from the assumption that you know nothing about computers and computer graphics. Later chapters will not be as detailed since you will have a working knowledge by then, making extended definitions and instruction unnecessary.

To work with DELUXEPAINT you will need to make two storage DISKS so that you can store or save any images that you create with the program. Do not save your pictures on the DELUXEPAINT program DISK. Of the two DISKS you are going to make, one DISK is for storing and the other is a backup DISK to copy the storage DISK. Follow this procedure: After turning on the computer, you insert the KICKSTART 1.1 DISK in the internal DISK drive when its request icon appears on the screen. After the WORKBENCH request icon appears, insert the WORKBENCH 1.1 DISK in the internal DISK drive. Insert a 3 and 1/2 inch, double-sided, double-density blank (unformatted) microdisk in the external DISK drive (if using a two drive system) after checking to see that the copy protect button is in the position that allows the DISK to receive information. Refer back to the introduction for details. Two DISK icons will appear on the MONITOR screen. One is for the WORKBENCH and the other is for the unformatted DISK which has a temporary NAME (DF1:BAD) since it is blank. Click the left mouse button once on the DF1:BAD icon to highlight it. Next, use the right mouse button to highlight INITIALIZE in the MENU by moving the mouse so that the arrow is on the word INITIALIZE and release the mouse button. The computer will inquire if you want to INITIALIZE DF1:BAD. Click the left mouse button on CONTINUE. The computer will format and verify the 80 cylinders (0 to 79) on the DISK. Do not remove the DISK while the red light is on. This formatted DISK will automatically be renamed EMPTY. Select RENAME from the MENU BAR at the top. Click the left mouse button in the NAME bar to activate it and use the KEYBOARD to delete its present name and rename your DISK. I name my storage DISKs:"dpvault1," "dpvault2" , etc., and the backup copies are named: "dpvault1.BAK," "dpvault2.BAK", etc.,... To save images to the storage DISK in the DPAINT programs you must have drawers to receive these images. Double-click on the icon of your storage DISK to open its window. Likewise, open the WORKBENCH window. In the WORKBENCH window, depress the left mouse button on the EMPTY drawer icon and drag it to your storage DISK window and release the left mouse button. Click the left mouse button on the EMPTY drawer in your DISK window and select RENAME with the right mouse button and change EMPTY's name to LO-RES. Select DUPLICATE from the MENU to make a copy of LO-RES. Rename this copy MED-RES. Copy MED-RES in like manner and rename it HI-RES. Copy HI-RES and rename it INTERLACE. Copy INTERLACE and rename it BRUSH. Use SNAPSHOT to position the icons in the window. Do not include any other spaces either before or after these names. This storage DISK can provide storage for about 40 LO-RES images of 20,000 kilobytes each totalling about 840,000 kilobytes. DUPLICATE this DISK to make your backup copy and rename it appropriately. Additional copies may be made of this storage DISK before anything is saved to it and each renamed as you wish.

To work with DELUXEPAINT when the computer is already operating under WORKBENCH you will need to reset the computer. To reset, (called a "warm boot") press the CTRL key and both red A's (Left Amiga closed and Right Amiga open which are on each side of the space bar) all at the same time. It takes two hands to do this. Never reset while the WORKBENCH DISK is being read by the DISK drive and the red light is on under the DISK drive. This will make the DISK unreadable.

If the computer is off, turn on the power and insert the KICKSTART 1.1 DISK when its request appears. After you reset or after you turn on the computer and insert the KICKSTART DISK the WORKBENCH DISK request will appear on the MONITOR screen. Do not insert the WORKBENCH. DELUXEPAINT includes WORKBENCH on its DISK so just insert the DELUXEPAINT DISK. The AmigaDos Command Line Interpreter screen will come up and the CLI prompt 1> will be onscreen.
                    Type: dpaint
                    Press: RETURN key

After about a minute the DELUXEPAINT title screen will appear and then the screen will literally turn blue and next the DELUXEPAINT screen and MENU will

appear. The screen will be black. Move the mouse
around and see how the cross hair lines respond to your
movement. If you move the cross hair lines into the
box of symbols on the right side of the screen called
the ICON CONTROL PANEL, the cross hair lines change
into an arrow pointer. Move the arrow over to the
black screen and press the left mouse button down and
hold it down while you move the mouse on a flat surface
and the cross hair lines will reappear and move
correspondingly on the black screen, drawing a white
line. Look at the color PAINT SET of four rows of
eight colors and greys on the right of the screen. In
LO-RES you have a choice of these 32 boxes of colors
and greys. At the top of the PAINT SET is a rectangle
with a circle in the middle. The rectangle shows which
color is being used as the background color. The
circle shows the color of the drawing point or brush as
this program calls them. To change the background
color, click with the right mouse button on any of the
32 boxes in the color set. The rectangle at the top of
the set will change to this color. If you want the
screen to be this color, click with the left mouse
button on the box named CLR which is above the
rectangle with a circle in it. This will clear the
screen and change the background color. To change the
color of your point or brush, click on any of the 32
boxes of color and the dot in the middle of the
rectangle at the top of the color set will change to
reflect your choice. KEYBOARD ([) and (]) picks the
next color up or down the set as the foreground color.
KEYBOARD (<) and (>) selects the next color up or down
the set as the background color.

You may change the amount of red, green or blue in
any of the 32 colors and greys. You may also adjust
the saturation and value to change the strength of the
color and make it lighter or darker. 4096 variations
of hue, saturation and value are available; however
only 32 may be used in any picture. If you change any
of the 32 boxes, anything previously colored with that
box of color will be changed as well. Here is how to
change a box in the PAINT SET. Use the right mouse
button to pull down the PICTURE MENU at the top of the
screen and continue to hold down the right button of
the mouse as you select COLOR CONTROL and then PALETTE.
Another way to do the same thing is to click with the
right mouse button on the circle in the rectangle at
the top of the PAINT SET which shows the current
foreground color of your point or brush. A third
option is to use the KEYBOARD and type a lower case
(p). Note that KEYBOARD commands will not work when

7

the pointer is on the ICON CONTROL PANEL or Title Strip
MENU BAR. Any of the three above mentioned actions has
the same result. A PALETTE appears on the screen. To
change any of the colors displayed in the PALETTE,
click with the left mouse button on its box in the
PAINT SET or click on its box in the PALETTE window.
To select a color from your screen image, click the
left mouse button on the circle in the rectangle at the
top of the PAINT SET or type the KEYBOARD command shown
in the following brackets: (,) and then move the POINT
to select an area of color on the screen by clicking
the left mouse button again. This is very useful when
you want to adjust a color that is nearly the same as
another.

In the PALETTE window you can move the slider
controls with the left mouse button held down as the
pointer moves the sliders. The R scale is the amount
of red in the color. Likewise the G scale is the
amount of green and B shows the amount of blue. Next
to the scales are controls for H for hue (color names),
S for saturation or purity of color and V for value or
the lightness or darkness of a color. These scales
also respond to the sliders. Numbers from 0 to 15
allow you to record the amounts of each mixture for
future selections of the same color. There is a box in
the PALETTE labelled UNDO. Click this with the left
mouse button to undo any change in the currently
selected color. Clicking the CANCEL box will undo
everything you have done in the PALETTE since opening
its window. You may move the PALETTE window around by
placing the pointer on its title bar and dragging the
PALETTE window to another location by holding down the
left mouse button and moving the mouse. The colors in
the PALETTE are numbered from 1 in the top left box to
32 in the bottom right box. The program will always
maintain some contrast between the colors in boxes 1
and 2 since these are the colors used for the lettering
and background on the screen. Boxes 17 through 20 are
used to draw the pointer and cross hair lines. If these
disappear it may be because of changes you have made in
the PALETTE. Other commands in the PALETTE include
COPY which allows you to first click on a color to be
copied and then click COPY and lastly, click on the
color which will be removed by the copy. A click on a
color and then on EX followed by a click on another
color will cause these colors to switch. This also
works in your image if you select an area of color and
click EX; then another area of a different color
causing the colors to exchange locations.

There are several other commands in the PALETTE window. If you click on a color and then click SPREAD before selecting another color, the computer will average the colors between the two selected. If you select box 3 and copy box 2 to box 32 you will get a spread of tints between the two boxes. The RANGE command determines the range between two boxes of color. It is used with SHADE, BLEND or CYCLE. Click the SH (SHADE) box and then click the color box to start the range. Next, click the RANGE box and finally the other box to set the range. Brackets will highlight the range. SHADE causes the brush to change a color it passes over to the next color above it in the set when the left mouse button is depressed while drawing. Depressing the right mouse button causes the next lower color in the PAINT SET to function. CYCLE causes a selected range of colors in the set to rotate in sequence at a speed determined by the slider control. Different ranges for cycling and different speeds may be assigned to each column in the PAINT SET by clicking on the boxes marked C1, C2 and C3. This concludes a survey of the options in the PALETTE window. If you want to use the changes you make in the PALETTE select the OK box and the PALETTE will disappear.

The numeric keypad or the KEYBOARD numbers 7 and 8 may be used to add to or subtract the amount of red in the current foreground color. The numbers 4 and 5 function the same way for green and the numbers 1 and 2 will shift the amount of blue in the color. The first two colors in the COLOR PALETTE (black and white) may be adjusted with the keys. Remember that these are the colors used to make the MENU titles. If you change these colors until you can not read the titles simply press the HELP key and the first color will return to black and the second color to white.

Now let us return to the ICON CONTROL PANEL. A click of the left mouse button on the box named UNDO or KEYBOARD (u) removes any activity of the mouse button since the last depression. Remember that KEYBOARD commands only work while the mouse cross hairs cursor is in the picture window. They will not work while the pointer is in the MENU BAR or ICON CONTROL PANEL. If you wish to work the full screen using the areas under the MENU BAR and ICON CONTROL PANEL press the (n) key which will scroll the image revealing the parts under the MENU BAR and ICON CONTROL PANEL. Using this method lets you make corrections with UNDO which would not be possible if you had removed these areas with the F9 and F10 FUNCTION KEYS. It is desirable to complete your

9

image in these areas or the printer will print black bands across the top and down the right side where the MENU BAR and ICON CONTROL PANELs occupy the screen. If you want to clear the screen and make it the current background color choice, select CLR with the left mouse button or KEYBOARD (K). Pressing the SPACE BAR allows you to change your mind in the middle of an action. Pressing the HELP key will take you back to the settings you started with. KEYBOARD (b) is like a left mouse button on a brush selection and KEYBOARD (B) is like a right mouse button on a brush selection.

The DELUXEPAINT program will start with a continuous freehand drawing tool of a single pixel, the smallest POINT possible on the screen in the current screen resolution. The built-in brushes have icons displayed at the top of the ICON CONTROL PANEL. Any of four round points and four square points along with three or five small points in a cluster may be chosen by clicking with the left mouse button while the pointer is displayed over the point. These points may be enlarged by selecting with the right mouse button and dragging the mouse while depressing either the left or right mouse button to enlarge or reduce the POINT size of the drawing tool, releasing the button when the size you want is achieved. The (=) or the (H) key on the KEYBOARD will also enlarge a brushpoint and the (-) or the (h) key will reduce the size of the brushpoint. A (.) will return to the one pixel brush. KEYBOARD commands are shown inside brackets. Do not type these brackets. Type the key shown and press the RETURN key.

To create an image, move the mouse and depress the left mouse button to color with the color in the circle in the rectangle at the top of the PAINT SET. The rectangle shows the color you will use if you press the right mouse button. This is an efficient way to DRAW and ERASE switching back and forth between foreground and background colors.

Under the BUILT-IN BRUSHES are four drawing tools. The DOTTED FREEHAND DRAWING tool will draw in a broken line with the distance between the dots determined by the speed of your moving the mouse. This allows a sketchy approach that looks somewhat like charcoal or pastel on rough paper when a cluster of points is used.

Note that any brush POINT may be used with any of the drawing tools and shape options.

The CONTINUOUS FREEHAND DRAWING tool is the tool that loads as the program starts and gives an unbroken line. This is the tool to use in drawing freehand shapes to be filled with a color using the FILL WITH COLOR command described below. Cluster points drawn with this tool look like cross-hatched pen and ink drawings. Large sized points make this tool sluggish as you move across the screen. Select FAST FEEDBACK with the right mouse button from the PREFS heading on the MENU BAR's top right and the program will DISPLAY a smaller POINT while drawing, expanding to the larger size as you continue your movement across the screen, completing the line in the size of your choice when you release the mouse button.

The STRAIGHT LINE tool will draw a straight LINE between the first depression of the mouse's left button to a POINT selected by moving the mouse and releasing the mouse button.

The CURVE tool draws a curved LINE when you click the left mouse button on a starting POINT and move the mouse to the ending POINT and release the mouse button. In this option the mouse cross hair lines will now act like a magnet attracting the curved LINE and forming different curves relative to the distance of the cross hair lines from the curve. When you make the curve of your choice, click the left mouse button while the mouse is at that position. Pressing SPACE BAR will stop drawing the curve during the action. To see the straight or curved LINE being drawn during the process press the CTRL key while drawing with the mouse using the STRAIGHT LINE or CURVE tool.

To select these tools from the KEYBOARD type (s) for the DOTTED FREEHAND LINE, (d) for CONTINUOUS FREEHAND LINE, (D) for one pixel LINE in CONTINUOUS DRAW,(v) for STRAIGHT LINE and (q) for CURVE.

For special EFFECTS you may use any of the drawing tools with the CYCLE draw option from the MODES MENU. Make the cycle range in the PALETTE window. To see the CYCLE EFFECT select CYCLE from the COLOR CONTROL option under the PICTURE MENU or press the TAB key.

Directly under the LINE tools are icons for the FILL WITH COLOR option which looks like a paint can spilling paint and the AIRBRUSH option which is like a spray nozzle. Use FILL WITH COLOR to flood FILL any shape completely bounded by a LINE or to change the color of any shape bounded by shapes of different

11

colors from a one pixel POINT to a full screen simply by clicking the left mouse button on the color of your choice in the PAINT SET and then clicking the left mouse button over the area you want to FILL. The KEYBOARD request for FILL WITH COLOR is (f). A click of the right mouse button fills with the current background color. AIRBRUSH places points selected from the BUILT IN BRUSH or brushes that you create described later on in this chapter in a pattern determined by the right mouse button. When you click the right mouse button on the AIRBRUSH icon you can adjust the size of the spray by moving the mouse releasing the mouse button when the appropriate size has been reached. The KEYBOARD request for AIRBRUSH is (a). Next, the panel presents four shape options. Any brush POINT may function in the shape options. Each shape option has an hollow (outline) or a filled (solid) aspect. The icon boxes are split diagonally. Click the left mouse button in the diagonal split of the desired aspect. At the left is RECTANGLE, KEYBOARD (r) for hollow and (R) for filled. When you select this shape, a depression of the left mouse button will stretch out a rectangle from that POINT to the POINT of releasing the mouse button. By pressing the SHIFT key during this procedure you can make a square. CIRCLE, KEYBOARD (c) for hollow and (C) for filled, is to the right and produces circles by clicking on a POINT which will be the center of your circle with the left mouse button and move the mouse to the desired radius. In the lower left, ELLIPSE, KEYBOARD (e) for hollow and (E) for filled, functions in the same way. POLYGON to the right starts where you click the left mouse button and connects lines between each click until you click the starting POINT or press the SPACE BAR. In the filled aspect it then fills the shape. If you press the SPACE BAR after drawing a couple of sides while drawing a filled polygon the computer will finish the polygon and fill it in. UNDO will remove a filled polygon but removes only the last line of a hollow polygon.

In the middle of the panel is a box with four triangles that look like corner tabs in photo albums. This BRUSH SELECTION TOOL is a powerful option which allows you to FRAME any portion of your screen image and use it as a brush. It can be from the size of one pixel to a full sized screen. This lets you custom design your own brushes. First, click with the left mouse button to choose this tool or KEYBOARD (b). Now, you can move to any area of your picture and again click the left mouse button, then drag out a box, releasing the button to select the area you want to use

12

as a brush. You may place this area, lifted from your picture, over any spot in your current picture or any other picture you LOAD to screen, by clicking the left mouse button when you have the location selected. A click of the right mouse button will remove that area from the screen. Any color that is the same as the current background color will be transparent when the left mouse button is clicked. To change the current background color place the pointer over the background color in the PAINT SET and click the right mouse button. After selecting a brush, if you switch to a built-in brush or make changes in you selected brush using the brush MENU subcommands (STRETCH, ROTATE ANY ANGLE or SHEAR) you can retrieve your brush by clicking the right mouse button or KEYBOARD (B). Any brush created in this fashion can be used to paint by pressing the left mouse button while moving the mouse. This tool also allows the copying of parts of one picture and using them in another picture. Simply select the area as a brush and then LOAD your other picture. When it comes on screen, a click of the left mouse button will drop a copy to the picture. Some color problems may occur if you are using two different PALETTEs for the two pictures. DELUXEPAINT can help. Go to the BRUSH MENU and choose CHANGE COLORS and then REMAP. The colors in the new PALETTE that are the closest to the colors in the PALETTE that created the brush will be selected automatically by the Amiga. You can override this color change by selecting USE BRUSH PALETTE under the COLOR CONTROL in the PICTURE MENU. Choose RESTORE PALETTE to undo the previous choice. If you have selected a multi-colored brush you can change one color by using CHANGE COLORS from the BRUSH MENU. Here is the procedure: Click with the right mouse button on the color in the PAINT SET you wish to change. Now, click your choice from the PAINT SET with the left mouse button. A selection of Bg->Fg from the MENU will switch the colors. A selected brush of a single color may be changed by selecting COLOR from the MENU and then picking a color from the PAINT SET.

Now, let us look at some other things to do to the brushes selected with the BRUSH SELECTION tool. Under the BRUSH MENU you will find SIZE with sub-menus: STRETCH, HALVE, DOUBLE, DOUBLE HORIZ and DOUBLE VERT.

STRETCH will cause the brush to enlarge or shrink relative to a movement of the mouse while either button is depressed. In addition, holding down the SHIFT key during this action will keep the brush in the same horizontal and vertical proportions.

HALVE reduces the brush one-half each time it is selected.

DOUBLE doubles the brush until this action would create a brush too large for the screen in which case the action will fail.

DOUBLE HORIZ doubles horizontally while keeping the vertical dimension constant.

DOUBLE VERT doubles vertically while keeping the horizontal dimension the same.

FLIP and sub-menu HORIZ or KEYBOARD (x) turns a brush around horizontally. Likewise, FLIP and sub-menu VERT or KEYBOARD (y) turns a brush upside-down.

ROTATE or KEYBOARD (z) allows clockwise rotation of 1/4 turn if you select the sub-menu 90 DEGREES. ANY ANGLE is controlled by either mouse button to rotate the box representing the brush to the desired angle and then releasing the button.

SHEAR lets you slide the bottom half of the selected brush to the left or to the right while the top half remains in position. Movement of the mouse while depressing the button affects the shearing.

Finally, BEND lets you select HORIZ for a horizontal bend or VERT for a vertical bend. The amount of the bend is controlled by dragging the mouse with either mouse button depressed releasing the button when the desired bend is accomplished.

The next box in the ICON CONTROL PANEL has an "A" in it and this stands for TEXT. A click of the left mouse button followed by another click of the left mouse button will position a text insertion box in the picture area. The KEYBOARD is used to ENTER text at that POINT using the current foreground color. Color may be changed from the PAINT SET for each individual letter, number or symbol. BACKSPACE key is used to ERASE characters in a line. If you want to start a NEW line at regular spacing use the RETURN key. You can place a NEW line anywhere with the mouse however; if you reposition the line of text with the mouse you will not be able to return to an earlier line and use the BACKSPACE to ERASE. You can place additional text next to the previous text. KEYBOARD (t) selects TEXT and the (ESC) key returns you to the paint program. Additional FONTS are available for loading from DISK.

Choose LOAD FONTS from the FONTS MENU. Choose from the list that appears. If you have not erased the picture "All fonts" from your program DISK you can LOAD this picture to see some of the font options. The currently selected font is shown in the FONTS MENU. Text may be selected with the BRUSH SELECTION tool and moved around the picture, changing its size, proportions and color just like any other brush. Drop shadows may be placed using the right mouse button to place the text in an appropriate background color for the shadow. By placing the text over this drop shadow and clicking the left mouse button the current foreground color will be visible on top of the shadow text.

The next box in the ICON CONTROL PANEL is a square divided into four smaller squares, a symbol for GRID which may be turned on with one click of the left mouse button or KEYBOARD (g). The GRID will stay active until you click again with the left mouse button on its icon. All tools except the CONTINUOUS FREEHAND LINE will conform to the GRID. For example: the intersections of the GRID lines are POINT to POINT (origin and termination) for straight and curved lines. A click of the right mouse button allows you to change the GRID. A click of the left mouse button displays the COORDINATES and dragging the mouse in the drawing area with the left mouse button depressed will alter the size of the GRID making it larger or smaller than the first GRID displayed. Release the left mouse button when the GRID is the size you want.

By drawing several boxes with the STRAIGHT LINE tool and lifting these boxes with the BRUSH SELECTION tool, then using DOTTED FREEHAND DRAWING you can paint a GRID over the picture area. You can make the GRID disappear after you use it to construct your image if you bring up the PALETTE window and COPY the background color to the box of the color with which you made the GRID. Any PATTERN lifted with the BRUSH SELECTION tool may be placed in multiples on a GRID filling the entire screen if you wish. A transparent GRID can be made on the SPARE screen (see below) and picked up as a BRUSH to return to the main screen and check relationships with a movable GRID which lets the picture show through.

Next door to GRID is the SYMMETRY box. A click of the left mouse button turns on this control or KEYBOARD (/) which remains active until you click again on its symbol with the left mouse button. Any of the other tools may be selected to work while SYMMETRY in on.

The ORDER of the symmetry can be altered by clicking on the SYMMETRY icon with the right mouse button to bring up the window. You can now choose any whole number up to 40 for the number of symmetry points to place in the ORDER box. ERASE any number appearing in the box using the BACKSPACE or the DELETE key before adding your new choice. The other options are MIRROR which draws lines in opposite directions around each symmetry POINT or CYCLIC which makes lines drawn at each symmetry POINT go in the same direction. The PICTURE MENU has a SYMMETRY CENTER which lets you select the center of the symmetry and set it by clicking the left mouse button. This NEW center will remain at this location until a NEW center is selected. This is true even if you turn off the SYMMETRY tool. Be cautious about extending complex symmetry designs beyond the screen limits. This may cause the program to "crash" and the pointer will refuse to move. You will lose the current work and will need to do a "warm boot" to start the program over.

MAGNIFY or KEYBOARD (m) is represented by a magnifying glass. Click the left mouse button to see a window on your picture screen that is an enlargement of your picture. A square will appear in your picture which can be moved over any area of the image with the mouse allowing you to select the enlarged area with a click of the left mouse button. Precise work may be done pixel by pixel. ZOOM is the box next to the MAGNIFY box and with ZOOM you can click the left mouse button, KEYBOARD (>), a number of times to zoom in on an area. Clicks of the right mouse button, KEYBOARD (<), zooms back out. Several views are possible with each zoom until the function stops and does not zoom in or out any further when you click the mouse button. The CURSOR DIRECTION ARROWS adjust the enlarged view over your image. KEYBOARD (n) recenters the picture. Click the left mouse button on the MAGNIFY box to return to your full screen image. This concludes a survey of the ICON CONTROL PANEL in LOW RESOLUTION.

There are some differences in working in MEDIUM RESOLUTION and HIGH RESOLUTION. In LOW RESOLUTION the screen measures 320 pixels across by 200 pixels down. A pixel is the smallest POINT possible on a screen. In MEDIUM RESOLUTION the screen measures 640 pixels across and 200 pixels down. In HIGH RESOLUTION the screen measures 640 pixels across by 400 pixels down. The smallest pixel in HIGH RESOLUTION is 1/4 the size of the smallest pixel in LOW RESOLUTION. To work in MEDIUM RESOLUTION after doing a "warm boot" or after

selecting QUIT from the PICTURE MENU type: (dpaint med)
at the 1> prompt and press the RETURN key . If you
have just turned on the computer, inserted KICKSTART,
removed KICKSTART, then, at the WORKBENCH request,
insert DELUXEPAINT DISK and at the 1> prompt type:
(dpaint med) and press the RETURN key. To select HIGH
RESOLUTION type: (dpaint hi) instead of (dpaint med)
following the above procedure. Both MEDIUM RESOLUTION
and HIGH RESOLUTION reduce the PALETTE to 16 colors.
Pictures created in one resolution may not be loaded
into another resolution; however, brushes may be saved
and moved from one resolution to another losing some of
the image in the transition. If a difference in
PALETTES changes the color in the transported brush,
use REMAP under the CHANGE COLORS option in the BRUSH
MENU to adjust the colors somewhat. Brushes selected
in MEDIUM and HIGH RESOLUTION may not be full screen
and large brushes may be shown as an empty FRAME until
the brush is placed in a position on the screen and
released with a click of the left mouse button. Any of
the sizing commands may fail if the size you select
would be too large for the screen. When working in
HIGH RESOLUTION the program will close WORKBENCH to
conserve memory. If you select QUIT from the PICTURE
MENU the program will restart.

    This next section will describe each of the MENU
options. Remember, to select MENU items press the
right mouse button and move the mouse to the right or
the left to highlight the option of your choice, then
release the right mouse button. Some of the options
have sub-menus which have options under their title as
well. The MENU BAR is at the top of the DPaint screen.
The first heading is PICTURE. Under PICTURE you can
select the following:

    LOAD = This will list the pictures stored on that
DISK at the current resolution. To see the entire
list, click the left mouse button on the arrows which
are on the side of the window or you can drag the
elevator bar up or down with a depressed left mouse
button to see titles which are off the screen. Place
the pointer over the name of the picture you want to
LOAD and click with the left mouse button. The name
will appear in the FILE SLOT. A click of the left
mouse button on LOAD will place it in memory and cause
it to come into view.

    SAVE = This should be chosen to SAVE the picture
that is on screen to the vault or storage DISK if it is
a picture that you have saved to a storage DISK from an

earlier time. If you LOAD a picture from memory and
do additional work on the picture, SAVE will store the
revised picture under the NAME of your earlier version.
The earlier version will be saved as well but will be
renamed BACKUP.PIC. This is a safety feature so that
if you make changes to a picture and SAVE it, you will
not lose your earlier version. If you want your
earlier version also, LOAD the BACKUP.PIC and use the
next option: SAVE AS... to give your picture its former
title. Be warned that each time you SAVE a picture
previously created and do not change the NAME of the
revision, the last work loaded will be placed under
BACKUP.PIC. This will lose forever an earlier image
that was placed in BACKUP.PIC and not renamed using
SAVE AS... which is described below.

SAVE AS... = This is the command to use to place a
picture on a storage DISK or vault. Do not store on
the DELUXEPAINT program DISK. Put the pointer over the
NAME box and click with the left mouse button. You can
NAME your picture by typing its NAME in the box. Use
the BACKSPACE and DELETE keys to correct any mistakes.
Press RETURN and click the left mouse button on SAVE.
Use SAVEAS... anytime you revise a work previously
saved with SAVEAS... if you want to save the first
version. For example: After you do your first picture
use SAVEAS... and NAME it say, PICTURE:A to save it to
a storage DISK. Now you can LOAD your first picture
named PICTURE:A from DISK. Revise PICTURE:A if you
wish and save the revision by selecting SAVEAS... and
naming the revision say, PICTURE:B. Each successive
stage can be saved and renamed with SAVEAS... This can
cause some confusion and you might think SAVE should be
used but remember that SAVE works like this: If you
named your first picture say, PICTURE:A and saved it to
DISK with SAVEAS... and then loaded PICTURE:A and
revised it, if you were to use SAVE, then your revision
would be given the NAME PICTURE:A and the first version
would be placed in BACKUP.PIC. If you use SAVE instead
of SAVEAS... you will keep losing the earlier
variations of your picture as BACKUP.PIC will hold only
the last version as a safety feature. Be sure you
understand the difference.

SYMMETRY CENTER = Sets the center for SYMMETRY
when you place the crosshairs on the screen with a
click of the left mouse button. The selected center
will stay there until you change it to another location
even if you turn SYMMETRY off and on again.

COLOR CONTROL = has sub-menus of:

PALETTE = Allows changes to the PAINT SET.

USE BRUSH PALETTE = Sets PALETTE to the one used to make a brush under BRUSH SELECTION.

RESTORE PALETTE = Undoes the above.

DEFAULT PALETTE = Sets PALETTE to the one that is used when the program starts.

CYCLE = Cycles colors selected to cycle in the PALETTE. Select again to turn off the cycling. Same as KEYBOARD (TAB).

SPARE = has these sub-menus:

SWAP or KEYBOARD (j) = There is another full screen behind the picture screen. This screen can be used to hold selected brushes, created patterns and other components of picture making. SWAP switches back and forth between the two screens.

PICTURE TO SPARE = Places the front screen image as a copy on the back screen.

MERGE IN FRONT = Any image placed on the spare screen will be made to appear on top of the front screen.

MERGE IN BACK = Any image placed on the spare screen will be made to appear behind the image on the front screen.

PATTERNS may be created on the spare screen. A painting on the front screen can have shapes filled with the PATTERN on the background screen by drawing with the background color (press right mouse button). When you select MERGE IN BACK the PATTERN will appear in the shapes drawn with the right mouse button.

The next command in this MENU is the PRINT command. If a printer is attached to the computer and it has been selected through PREFERENCES in the WORKBENCH select PRINT with the right mouse button and after a few moments the printer will print the image on screen. A background color border will print on the top and right side of your picture. If you want these

19

borders to be the color of your paper you can use the
F9 and F10 FUNCTION KEYS to remove the MENU BAR and the
ICON CONTROL PANEL. If you have selected the FILL WITH
COLOR command and white as the color, you can FILL the
top and side borders by clicking the left mouse button
while the symbol for the FILL WITH COLOR is in the
area.

QUIT is the command to pick when you wish to EXIT
the DELUXEPAINT program.

Next to the PICTURE MENU is the BRUSH MENU. To
LOAD a brush from a DISK choose LOAD under the BRUSH
MENU. Click with the left mouse button on the NAME of
the drawer you wish to select. A list of the available
brushes will be shown. Click with the left mouse
button on the NAME of the brush and then on LOAD.
Drawers are changed by clicking the left mouse button
on the horizontal bar containing the current drawer's
name. Replace this NAME using BACKSPACE and DEL keys;
then type in the NAME of the drawer of choice and press
the RETURN key. The other MENU choices under BRUSH
have already been described.

Moving to the right, the next heading in the MENU
BAR is MODES. It contains these commands:

OBJECT = displays the selected brush as it was
when it was created.

COLOR = changes all the colors in a brush to the
foreground color except for the transparent color or
the background color at the time of selection.

REPLACE = gives the brush colors at the time of
creation plus the transparent color is now visible.

SMEAR = pushes color from the area where you begin
to depress the left mouse button into the surrounding
area until you release the left mouse button. The
EFFECT diminishes as the distance from the starting
POINT increases.

SHADE = uses a range chosen from the PALETTE. A
click of the left mouse button on SH lets you pick the
color at one end of the range, then RANGE is clicked
and finally the color is clicked with the left mouse
button on the color that represents the other end of
the range. Brackets will show the RANGE of SHADE.
This mode lets you use a brush to change any color the
brush passes over into the next highest color in the

20

PAINT SET if you are employing the left mouse button. However, the right mouse button will choose the next lowest color. Colors out of range will not be affected.

BLEND = averages the colors in the selected range as a brush moves over the screen.

CYCLE = lets you cycle draw with a brush in a selected range of colors.

When selected, FONTS will LOAD the text FONTS. LOAD ALLFONTS to see the choices.
PREFS is the last MENU heading. It has three options:

BRUSH HANDLE = does a switch between holding a selected brush in the center or apparently holding the selected brush by the lower right-hand corner. The choice is made before the brush is created. To change the orientation, just pick this option again before making another brush.

COORDINATES = gives the location of the xy coordinates on the right side of the MENU BAR relative to the top left of the of the image screen when the mouse is moved without depressing a button. By pressing the left mouse button and dragging the mouse, the xy is reset to 0,0 and the MENU BAR displays numbers relating to the movement of the mouse away from selected points.

FAST FEEDBACK = is used to let line and hollow shape tools to be drawn rapidly in a smaller brush size until the mouse button is released. At that time the line or shape will be redrawn in the size of the current brush.

In addition, there are ten FUNCTION KEYS:
F1 = OBJECT
F2 = COLOR
F3 = REPLACE
F4 = SMEAR
F5 = SHADE
F6 = BLEND
F7 = CYCLE
F8 = CURSOR CROSS-HAIRS ON/OFF
F9 = MENU BAR ON/OFF
F10 = ICON CONTROL PANEL ON/OFF

Pressing these FUNCTION KEYS has the same effect as selecting a MENU item with the right mouse button. The other KEYBOARD commands are:

ALT+OPEN AMIGA = right mouse button
ALT+CLOSED AMIGA = left mouse button
CTRL = leaves traces while drawing with the line or hollow shape tools. Depress this key while drawing.

This concludes a survey of the DELUXEPAINT program.

CHAPTER THREE

USING DELUXEPAINT II

In December of 1986, Electronic Arts released an upgraded version of DELUXEPAINT. This program is similar to the original program with the following exceptions.

DELUXEPAINT II requires that you use KICKSTART 1.2 instead of the earlier version 1.1. The program will LOAD and the INTUITION window will open. Double-click on the DPaint icon and again on the paintcan icon for dpaint. Note that a new drawer has been added for the INTERLACE mode. After a few seconds the SCREEN FORMAT requester will appear. You may select these options:

        LO-RES (320x200 pixels)
        MED-RES (640x200 pixels)
        INTERLACE (320x400 pixels)
        HI-RES (640x400 pixels)

and the number of available PALETTE colors 2, 4, 8, or 16. All 32 colors may be used only in LO-RES unless you have additional memory above 512k in which case 32 colors may be used in the INTERLACE mode. Additional memory is also required for 16 colors in HI-RES. You are given the option of LOAD ALL which will LOAD the entire program into memory or you may choose SWAP which will require loading portions of the program from time to time as required but saves some memory. This version needs a lot of memory to use all the new functions. One or two megabytes is recommended. CTRL/A will show you the amount of memory at any time. Click the right mouse button on the MENU BAR to get the MENU back. Once you have made your choices select OK or CANCEL to return to the main MENU.

The MENU BAR and ICON CONTROL PANEL will look familiar. Some additions to the ICON CONTROL PANEL are that a click of the right mouse button on the STRAIGHT LINE or the CURVED LINE will open a SPACING requester. If you select RELATIVE with a click of the left mouse button and set the NUMBER box a STRAIGHT LINE or CURVED LINE (whichever you opened) can be drawn composed of the same number of dots as the defined NUMBER. These dots will be spaced out over the length of the LINE. If you select ABSOLUTE the LINE will have a distance between dots of the NUMBER of pixels selected in the NUMBER box. This option is turned ON and OFF by clicking the left mouse button on the respective boxes.

23

Pick OK to return to the screen or CANCEL to undo this option.

If you click the right mouse button on the FILL icon a FILL TYPE requester opens. A click of the left mouse button on the SOLID box will FILL the screen with a selected color. PERSPECTIVE will place a selected brush in a PERSPECTIVE FILL. PATTERN lets you FILL geometric solids with a selected PATTERN. FROM BRUSH selects a PATTERN from a captured brush. GRADIENT will FILL vertically, horizontally or by boundary LINE depending on which box of directional arrows is selected. DITHER is the amount of blending of the pixels. A slider controls the amount of DITHER. The colors in the GRADIENT FILL are selected from the COLOR CONTROL PANEL.

Two clicks on the BRUSH icon will let you click around any shape to use as a captured BRUSH. You no longer have to be content with rectangular BRUSHES. A click of the right mouse button on SYMMETRY icon opens its requester. POINT sets a POINT around which the symmetry is arranged in the usual CYCLIC or MIRROR design. The ORDER determines the number of points of symmetry and PLACE sets the center of the symmetry. TILE lets you set the WIDTH and HEIGHT of a TILE PATTERN. A captured brush will TILE the screeen replicating itself.

Pull down the DELUXEPAINT MENU options with the right mouse button. LOAD will now allow mouse selection of the DF0:, DF1: or DH: drive. DF0: is the internal drive. DF1: is the external and DH: is a hard drive. Once selected, the DIRECTORY and list of pictures available for loading will show in the window. To select, click with the left mouse button on the NAME of the picture and click also on LOAD. SAVE works the same way as does DELETE, a new feature that allows you to remove pictures from your DISK. SYMMETRY CENTER is no longer under this MENU but is under the EFFECTS heading and renamed CENTER. PRINT opens up the PRINT PICTURE window. Here you can choose the ORIENTATION of the picture making it either NORMAL or SIDEWAYS. SHADE offers B&W for black and white, GREY and COLOR boxes. MARGINS provides the means of changing the various margins of the print and NUMBER OF COPIES can be set for multiple copies. Under COLOR CONTROL there are four color CYCLE ranges and the direction and speed of the CYCLE can be set. A new item under SPARE is DELETE THIS PAGE. PAGE SIZE is for setting the size by typing in the pixels from 320 x 200 up to 1024 x 1024 or selecting one of the three boxes. STANDARD is 320 x 200, FULL PAGE is 320 x 340 and is like working on the top or bottom half of a sheet of paper. Select SHOW PAGE with the right mouse button to see a reduced version of the larger image. Note that some points are dropped out in these reductions but if you print your image it will look like the two halves put together. There is some overlapping between the top and bottom to assist you in relating the two halves. SHOW PAGE may be picked by KEYBOARD (S). Note that this is a capital S and not lower case. FULL VIDEO paints a picture all the way to the edge of the screen which is especially helpful when combining images with video and video production using GENLOCK. GENLOCK is hardware which permits the overlaying of computer images and lettering on top of a video image. This combination may be videotaped. DELUXEPAINT lets you switch from one SCREEN FORMAT to another without starting up the program again by selecting SCREEN FORMAT. A window called CHOOSE SCREEN FORMAT lets you transport your image into another format. To use the 32 colors of INTERLACE or the 16 colors in HI-RES additional memory above 512k is required. The computer will create a new PALETTE when a color image with a larger PALETTE (say 32 colors) is changed to a format which reduces the number of colors. SCREEN SIZE PAGE on or KEEP SAME PAGE are other options in this sub-menu. If your image is larger than the screen size you may use the scroll arrows to move around your picture. A change in format can alter the proportions of your picture. A 320 x 200 LO-RES picture changed to a 320 x 400 will look too elongated vertically. The next item in the sub-menu list is ABOUT which tells who wrote this excellent program. Following that is the last choice in this list: QUIT which exits the DELUXEPAINT program.

BRUSH MENU now has DELETE as a sub-menu and the HANDLE command is moved to this MENU.

The MODE MENU has a new NAME for a captured brush. Formerly called OBJECT the new NAME is MATTE. A MATTE brush has a transparent background. A new option is SMOOTH which reduces the "jaggies" of the sharp edges of contrasting pixels blending them with colors from the current PALETTE. It gives effects that look like watercolor where water has been flooded into a wash or like the dissolve of turpentine on oil paint. It is very handy to lower the definition of the chosen area or to soften the boundaries of areas. There is no KEYBOARD call for SMOOTH.

The fun begins with a new item under EFFECTS called STENCIL. The KEYBOARD command is the tilde (~) sign under the (ESC) key. This EFFECT protects selected colors from being "painted over." Here is an example of how it works. After you open the STENCIL requester window you will see the following boxes. First, is a box named LOCK which when clicked with the left mouse button will let you select those colors to be locked or not to be painted over. Click the left mouse button on as many colors as you wish. Colors may also be selected from your image area as in the original DELUXEPAINT. For our example we will pick only black. Notice that a black tab on the right of the chosen color will now appear. Click the left mouse button on the MAKE box to use the current selected color or colors. If you change your mind, select CANCEL. CLEAR will remove the LOCK from all colors. In our example, we can draw with the black. Any of the other colors will paint behind the black. If we return to the STENCIL requester window we can now pick the INVERT box and again click on MAKE. Now pick one of the colors and say, AIRBRUSH as your brush. If you spray in the black area now, only the black area will receive the AIRBRUSH dots. Another example will show some of the other options under STENCIL. Again LOCK black and click MAKE. Pick the FILLED CIRCLE from the ICON CONTROL PANEL and make a circle. Next, select REVERSE from the STENCIL sub-menu and click the left mouse button on CLR to clear the screen. Any colors you use now will FILL up the original circle. Shapes from captured brushes may be pasted on the screen but only the part defined by the original circle will appear. REMAKE lets you create a new shape and FIX FG sets the original locked colors. ON/OFF turns the STENCIL on or off. FREE removes the STENCIL options from the current operations. LOAD, SAVE and DELETE complete the sub-menus under STENCIL.

The new BACKGROUND FIX freezes the current image that is onscreen and you may make changes on top of this image, remove "brush" shapes created on top of the image, and by selecting CLR return to the original unchanged image. A digitized photograph might be fixed with this command and a black contour drawing done on top of the digitized image and removed as a brush to a spare screen and saved to DISK. The original image would not be altered. FREE releases the FIX.

The most dramatic addition to this updated version of DELUXEPAINT is the PERSPECTIVE command under the EFFECTS MENU. Any brush can be plotted as if if was floating in space. CENTER is chosen to place a POINTtoward which parallel lines appear to converge. After you set the center, select PERSPECTIVE DO to put the brush in an area of the screen. You will now see a window with four sections which will respond to the movements of the mouse. This combined with the KEYBOARD number pad lets you pick the x (7 or 8), y (4 or 5) and z (1 or 2) angles of the rotation of the window plane representing your brush image. Now if you press the number keys you will see the change of plane in your image. The 3, 6, and 9 keys reset each shift in angle to the flat plane. KEYBOARD (0) resets all and the (ENTER) key puts you in the PERSPECTIVE mode. ANTI-ALIAS is used to smooth out the brush image since some "jaggies" or stepped edges occur as pictures are shifted in PERSPECTIVE. This is a slow process taking about five minutes for a complex image. NONE can be the choice if the edges are not a problem and you are impatient. Select LOW or HIGH to see the EFFECT of the smoothing out of ANTI-ALIAS. ABSOLUTE or RELATIVE ROTATION are the final options under PERSPECTIVE.

FONTS have some larger sizes and the added BOLD, ITALIC and UNDERLINE styles.

PREFERENCES offers MULTICYCLING which lets the cycled colors move in more than one direction. BE SQUARE adjusts a drawn circle or square so that it is truly a circle or square allowing for the pixel aspect ratios. Formerly, circles or squares would be slightly extended vertically. EXCLBRUSH assists in PATTERN making by computing the edges of square brushes placed on grids so that they fit uniformly.

The MINUS sign (-) and the (=) sign let you reduce and enlarge brushes. You can now reduce a brush gradually and enlarge it back to its former size or even make it larger with no breakup of the pixels. F10 function key now removes both the MENU BAR and ICON CONTROL PANEL.

DELUXEPAINT is a fine tool for the artist. DELUXEPAINT II maintains this excellence and adds many desirable functions.

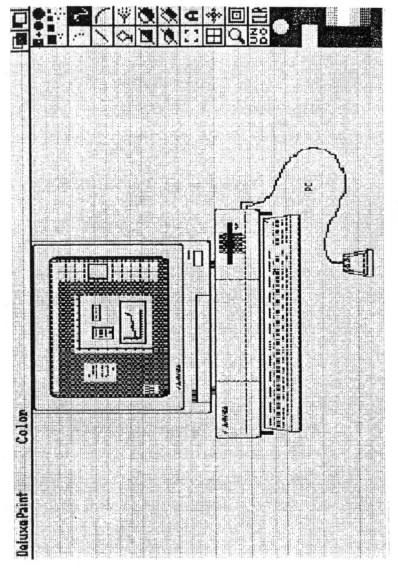

The monitor screen displaying DELUXEPAINT's menu.

CHAPTER FOUR

USING GRAPHICRAFT

GRAPHICRAFT was the first paint program available
for the Amiga. It is a fine program that is easy to
learn with its relatively simple commands. It does not
have all of the different options of the other paint
programs, but the ones it has will allow some complex
pictures to be made including cycle animation. Most of
the commands are from the MENU BAR and only a few
KEYBOARD commands are possible, thus simplifying the
procedure. The following instructions will give you a
good introduction to this program.

GRAPHICRAFT is loaded after KICKSTART 1.1 and
WORKBENCH have been loaded. WORKBENCH is not included
on the GRAPHICRAFT disk. When the GRAPHICRAFT icon
appears, double-click on the icon with the left mouse
button. If you prefer, you may LOAD GRAPHICRAFT from
the CLI (Command Line Interpreter) by typing:
(GRAPHICRAFT) at the 1> prompt. When the window opens,
double-click with the left mouse button on the
GRAPHICRAFT PALETTE icon and the screen will open. The
MENU BAR is at the top of the screen and has the
following options which are pulled down into view and
selected with the right mouse button.

The first MENU heading on the left is PROJECT.
Under PROJECT you can select these commands:

NEW = clears the screen to the default background
color which is white in this program.

OPEN = allows you to LOAD either PAINTINGS or
BRUSHES by clicking the left mouse button on either
PAINTING or BRUSH and then clicking the left mouse
button on the NAME of a PAINTING or BRUSH that you have
saved to DISK or a demo on a program DISK. You may
also type its NAME in the TITLE box if you prefer.
Next, click the left mouse button on the OK box to
LOAD or the CANCEL box if you change your mind.

REVERT = After you have worked on a picture and
you do not want to save the new version, select this
option to go back to the way your picture looked when
first loaded.

SHOW TITLE BAR = displays the MENU BAR at the top
of the screen.

HIDE TITLE BAR = makes the MENU BAR disappear. It is still active and you may make selections by placing the : r symbol in the area at the top of the screen and pressing the right mouse button. MENU options will appear while the right mouse button is depressed over their locations in the MENU.

PRINT = sends the current picture to the printer.

QUIT = exits the program and sends you back to the WORKBENCH window.

The next MENU heading is EDIT. It has these commands:

UNDO = removes the last action. KEYBOARD: (Right Amiga A + Q) does the same.

FRAME = click the left mouse button, drag and release to FRAME an area before you ERASE, CUT, COPY or PASTE.

CUT = removes an area bounded by a FRAME. The screen area cut by the FRAME will change to the background color. The KEYBOARD command for this is: (Right Amiga A + X). CUT works after FRAME.

COPY = after FRAME, selects an area for cloning. The KEYBOARD command is: (Right Amiga A + C).

PASTE = allows you to place a FRAME CUT or a FRAME COPY at a location determined by clicking the left mouse button and dragging the FRAME to its place and then releasing the left mouse button. Press the right mouse button to remove the FRAME border LINE. The KEYBOARD command is: (Right Amiga A + V).

ERASE = removes anything that you have enclosed in a FRAME leaving the background color.

ERASE SCREEN = removes all but the background color. It will ask if you want to lose the current picture. If you do, select YES with a click of the left mouse button. If you change your mind you can continue to work on the picture or do a SAVE AS after clicking the left mouse button on CANCEL.

The next MENU heading is SPECIAL. From this you will be able to pull down these options:

MAGNIFY = has two command options:

PICK POSITION = will move the crosshair cursor by depressing the left mouse button and dragging the cursor to the area you want to MAGNIFY. PICK POSITION with a click of the left mouse button. The DRAG BAR on top of the window moves the FRAME. Depress the left mouse button, drag and release to enlarge or reduce an area of magnification. After two clicks of the left mouse button the cursor POINTwill deposit the current brush color in a selected magnified GRID square. A click of the left mouse button on the gadget (box in the upper left of the FRAME) will close MAGNIFY or you can select MAG OFF with the right mouse button.

CONTINUOUS = will function with a click of the left mouse button on an area of your picture allowing you to drag out the window by depressing the left mouse button on the lower right corner. Click the left mouse button on the area you wish to MAGNIFY. The active GRID square will be outlined. Locate this GRID square for a change of color. Click the left mouse button to change the GRID square to the current brush color. A click of the left mouse button on close gadget or right mouse button on MAG OFF will cease the function.

MIRRORS = lets you select the number of VERTICAL and HORIZONTAL MIRRORSs by clicking the left mouse button on the number in the DISPLAY and then depressing the DEL key on the KEYBOARD. Now, type in any number from 1 to 9. BACK SPACE to correct errors. You may also choose DIAGONAL MIRRORS. When you have made your choice, click the left mouse button on YES or NO. When through with this window click the left mouse button on OK to use your settings or choose CANCEL if you decide not to use MIRROR. MIRROR OFF will stop the MIRROR function. Experiment with the various settings to see the numerous possibilities of this option.

CYCLE DRAW = will DISPLAY a window. By depressing the left mouse button on the solid box in the horizontal bar of the CYCLE' SPEED you can alter the speed of the cycling. Click the left mouse button on the color box that will be the first color in the CYCLE. Next, click the RANGE box and then click the last color of the CYCLE, with the left mouse button. BACK moves the CYCLE back one box. This creates an on-off EFFECT or a zig-zag. Select OK with the left mouse button or CANCEL to exit the window. Any BRUSH you select to work with will progress through the CYCLE you determined in the window options. Depress the right mouse button on CYCLE DRAW OFF to stop CYCLE DRAW.

CYCLE COLORS = allows the same kinds of selection as CYCLE DRAW and when this option is in EFFECT any colors picked will cycle. Click the left mouse button on OK to see the CYCLE or CANCEL. CYCLE COLORS OFF turns off the cycling.

The next heading in the MENU is COLOR. Pull down the window with the right mouse button and release the right mouse button on the COLOR you want to use with your BRUSH. If you release the button on the CHANGE PALETTE box a window will open displaying the current BRUSH COLOR in the large rectangle on the left. Click the left mouse button on any of the other colors to alter them or you may alter the current BRUSH COLOR. The R is the amount of red in the COLOR. The G is the amount of green and the B is the amount of blue. By placing the cursor over the slider bar and dragging the bar you can change these amounts. COPY will change a box to a COLOR picked by clicking the left mouse button on your choice, click the same button on COPY and then on the destination box. RANGE averages the COLORS between your first choice and your second. Use the left mouse button to click RANGE, then the COLORS. OK sets the PALETTE and CANCEL exits without changing the PALETTE. Be cautious of changing the first two colors so that there is a lack of contrast between them since these are the colors used to DISPLAY the Menus.'

SHAPE is the MENU heading containing the actions performed by the BRUSH you select. The curved LINE is for continuous free-hand drawing. The straight LINE, when active, will draw a straight LINE from one click of the left mouse button until a second click. Under the curved LINE is a symbol for BOUNDARY FILL. When active, it will FILL any shape bounded by a continuous LINE with the current BRUSH COLOR. The rectangle will draw squares or rectangles after clicking the left mouse button on the POINT where the upper left corner will be. Move the mouse to stretch out the shape to the POINT of the lower right corner and click the left mouse button on this point. Circles of various sizes are made by clicking the left mouse button on the center POINT of the circle and moving the mouse until the size of the circle grows to the size you want in your work, then click the left mouse button.

TEXT = lets you use the KEYBOARD to enter TEXT in two FONTS. Select TEXT with the left mouse button.

Next, you will see in a window samples of the FONTS. Select from the three types. The first will give TEXT in the color shown on top of any area where you type. The middle type will print in the color shown surrounded by the color as displayed. The last on the right will print black TEXT on any background selected. To change the colors, click the left mouse button on the TEXT box and then on the color box of your choice. To change the border in the middle DISPLAY so that a different color will be in the space block around your letters click the left mouse button on the SPACE box, then click the left mouse button on the background color of your choice. To use the changes you have made click the left mouse button on the OK box or click the left mouse button on the CANCEL box to return to the main MENU without making any changes. Note that you will have to select a brush or other option to leave the TEXT mode.

    The last MENU option is BRUSH. When this is selected a window appears with the available brush choices. The first on the left is the one-pixel brush. All the others are like they look. To pick one of these brushes, release the right mouse button on the box containing the brush POINT that you want. If you want to design your own brush point, release the right mouse button on CUSTOM BRUSH. In this window you may COPY any POINT by clicking the left mouse button on the POINT that you want to copy. Next click the left mouse button on the COPY box and next, click the left mouse button on the box of the POINT that you wish to replace with the copy. Alterations in the copy may be made by clicking the left mouse button on the large white or red squares and then draw pixel by pixel to change the brush in the EDIT window. This new brush may be deposited in any of the brush boxes. If you click the left mouse button on white or red boxes at the bottom and then click the left mouse button on the FILL box the EDIT box will be filled with that color. Again, you can use either the red or white color to draw a brush in the EDIT box. The four pointers allow you to vary the position of the brush relative to the box edges. Click the left mouse button on the pointer direction you desire. By clicking the left mouse button on OK you return to the main MENU with your custom brushes. You will need to select the brush you want to use, however. If you change your mind and do not want to use the custom brushes select the CANCEL box with a click of the left mouse button. If you open BRUSHES from the MENU, a window will show you brush files. If POINTERS or FOOTPRINTS is in the DIRECTORY you may pick one of these by clicking the left mouse button on the NAME of your choice.

In conclusion, I have found that the mouse is very responsive in GRAPHICRAFT. In other words, it draws fast with no delay. I hope you enjoy working with this program.

The monitor screen displaying AEGIS IMAGES' menu.

35

CHAPTER FIVE

USING AEGIS IMAGES

Aegis IMAGES is mainly a mouse-driven graphic program with only a few KEYBOARD commands. It has many of the same functions as the other programs and some that are unique. It is the most complex system described in this book and presents the artist with numerous fine tools with which excellent work can be created in the LOW RESOLUTION mode.

First, make a working copy of the IMAGES disk. There is not enough memory left on this DISK to save much work so you should initialize storage DISKs for saving your pictures. It is not necessary to create drawers like LO-RES.

IMAGES is loaded after KICKSTART 1.1. It has WORKBENCH on its DISK. To open the IMAGES disk click on the DISK icon with the left mouse button. A window will appear. In this window you should double-click the left mouse button on the IMAGES icon or click the left mouse button once on the icon and choose OPEN from the PROJECT MENU. If you prefer using the CLI you may type IMAGES at the 1> prompt. In a few moments the IMAGES screen will be visable.

The TITLE bar or MENU BAR is at the top of the screen. Depress the right mouse button to see the MENU headings. MENU selections are made by depressing the right mouse button while dragging the cursor until it is on the MENU option and then releasing the right mouse button. Sub-menu options are selected in the same fashion.

A window is on the lower left of the screen. This is called the FAST MENU and contains the current color PALETTE and the last three brushes and shapes you have chosen to work with. PATTERNS are also shown. This FAST MENU allows onscreen selection of these items without returning to the top of the screen to the main MENU if you prefer working in this manner. You may select by clicking the left mouse button on the box of your choice. The FAST MENU is not fully open when it appears so use the control at the lower right to reveal the full window by stretching it out. The DRAG BAR lets you move the FAST MENU to another screen location. The close gadget at the upper left closes this window. To re-open, select FAST MENU from the MENU BAR.

The PROJECT MENU heading has these options. The first is OPEN which opens a PAINTING, a WINDOW (a portion of a PAINTING like a BRUSH in DELUXEPAINT) or COLOR (PALETTE) stored on a DISK. PAINTINGS are the full image stored on a DISK with the extension .pic so a PAINTING would have a period and the letters pic attached to the end of its name. Likewise, a WINDOW has the extension .win attached to its NAME and a COLOR will have .col at the end. To OPEN one of these, position the cursor so that a sub-menu PAINTING, WINDOW or COLOR is chosen and release the right mouse button. If there are any saved images in the FILE a requester box will appear listing the available choices. Put the cursor on the title of the image you want to LOAD and click the left mouse button. The image should appear. If you choose COLOR and START the default color PALETTE for IMAGES will load.

The next option is SAVE AS and may be chosen to save a PAINTING, a WINDOW or a COLOR to DISK. In the requester window use the KEYBOARD to type in the NAME of your PICTURE, WINDOW or COLOR. Do not type the extensions as these will be added automatically. Images will be saved to the current DIRECTORY so if you have a storage DISK in another drive you must direct the computer by changing the DIRECTORY to the destination drive or NAME the storage DISK if you are using one drive. See the next paragraph about changing directories.

To change the current DIRECTORY select CHANGE DIRECTORY from the PROJECT MENU. When the requester appears, type in the NAME of the desired DISK or DIRECTORY and press the RETURN key. If for example you want an external drive you might type:
                    df1: <RETURN>
Following this item is the SHOW TITLE BAR which makes the MENU heading visable at the top of the screen. After you become familiar with the MENU headings you may opt to HIDE TITLE BAR making it invisible.

FAST MENU returns this tool if you have removed it from the screen.

PRINT PICTURE sends the current screen image to the printer if one is attached to the computer. Be sure the printer options are set in the PREFERENCES window of the WORKBENCH for the appropriate settings for your picture. PRINTER SET lets you select the size and proportions of your print.

LOCK will lock a brush or a shape in the FAST MENU window. First select LOCK and then click the left mouse button on the brush or shape you want in the FAST MENU. To undo the chosen brush or shape choose UNLOCK.

QUIT exits the IMAGES program. The KEYBOARD command is (Right Amiga A + Q).

EDIT is the next MENU heading. Under EDIT you may select UNDO which reverts back to the image before the last tool was used. This action is not like the UNDO of other programs which just undoes the last action of the mouse. This UNDO will remove all the marks made by the last tool chosen back to the time of its selection. The KEYBOARD command is (Right AMIGA A + V).

FRAME lets you define a rectangular area by placing the cursor on one corner and after clicking the left mouse button you can drag the cursor to the other corner and click the left mouse button a second time. The area inside this rectangular FRAME may now be altered by tool icons on the FRAME. To move the FRAME put the cursor on a border of the FRAME and click the left mouse button. This causes the FRAME to move wherever the mouse cursor moves. A second click of the left mouse button will place the image in the FRAME in the location of your choice. To PASTE a FRAME image click with the left mouse button on the (P) icon in the lower left of the FRAME. The icon in the upper right corner is for rotating the image in the FRAME. By clicking the left mouse button on this icon you cause a ghost FRAME to appear. You can now move the mouse any direction to rotate your image any angle. A second click of the left mouse button will deposit the rotated image on the screen. The image in the FRAME may be enlarged or reduced by selecting the resize icon in the lower right corner. Mouse movements will stretch or shrink the image. A second click of the left mouse button will place the resized image on the screen. A click of the left mouse button on the (x) in the upper left will cancel a FRAME selection.

To paint with a captured area in a FRAME put the cursor on the inside of the FRAME and depress the left mouse button and draw with the contents of the FRAME. The FRAME will disappear while you are moving the mouse but will return when you release the left mouse button.

Any image placed in a FRAME may be saved to DISK with SAVE AS. Later, these saved images may be loaded and placed in your pictures. With the right mouse button select SAVE AS and WINDOW from the PROJECT heading in the MENU BAR. Put the cursor on a corner of the FRAME and click the left mouse button. Next, mark the opposite corner and click the left mouse button a second time. When the FILE requester appears, use the KEYBOARD to type the NAME of your FRAME and press (RETURN). Your FRAME will be saved as a WINDOW.

A WINDOW may be loaded into your picture by selecting OPEN and WINDOW from the PROJECT MENU BAR. When the WINDOW requester appears pick the WINDOW of your choice by placing the cursor on its NAME and clicking once with the left mouse button. A FRAME containing the image will be active on the screen and all the FRAME options may be invoked.

CLEAR SCREEN does just that, removing everything on the current screen and presents the current background color as the screen. The KEYBOARD command is (Right AMIGA A + Z). A requester box will let you cancel the CLEAR SCREEN if you change your mind.

SWAP SCREENS brings the spare screen in front. The KEYBOARD command is (Right AMIGA A + S). It is totally separate from the first screen and provides a handy alternate work area. Images may be loaded to the spare screen and a FRAME from the front screen may be pasted on the back spare screen image.

MAGNIFY will enlarge a specific area so that you can work with greater accuracy. The KEYBOARD command is (Right AMIGA A + K). The magnified area may be resized by using the resize option on the lower right corner of the MAGNIFY window. The elevator bar on the side may be moved to zoom in or zoom out on the magnified area. A click of the left mouse button on the MOVE AREA corner will allow you to move the window over other areas of the screen image. First, observe where you are in the image. Next, position the cursor on the area you want to MAGNIFY and depress the left mouse button. The FRAME will jump to the new area. Moving the cursor with the left mouse button depressed now will allow precise positioning of the FRAME. When over the chosen spot, release the left mouse button. To end the MAGNIFY option select the close gadget in the upper left corner or select with the left mouse button on MAGNIFY OFF in the MENU.

Under the SPECIAL MENU heading are a number of special EFFECTS that make IMAGES a versatile program.

The first special EFFECT is WASH. This blends the
colors in an image producing results that resemble
watercolor washes or dissolves in oil painting where
paint thinner is used to spread and blend areas of
color.   WASH works with the colors in the current
PALETTE averaging the borders where colors meet.   This
will softens any lines and smooth the edges of shapes.
To use WASH you select the command from the SPECIAL
MENU with the right mouse button. Put the cursor over
the area that will be "washed" or blended.   The brush
choice directly relates to the WASH EFFECT. You may
work with just one pixel or you may blend with a large
brush.   The WASH occurs under the area of the brush.
Press down the left mouse button and move the mouse
over the places you want to smooth out. Several passes
over the same area will add to the WASH EFFECT.   WASH
will continue until you release the left mouse button
and pick another action like a shape from the SHAPE
MENU heading.

SMEAR also averages the colors under the brush
using the current PALETTE of colors but the colors are
reduced to one color.   Brush selection gives vastly
different results with SMEAR. It functions like WASH
in that you depress the left mouse button and move the
mouse to place the cursor over the areas to SMEAR.
SMEAR will function also until the left mouse button is
released and another action is selected.

CYCLE COLORS works with a range of colors selected
from the current PALETTE and cycles through the
selected range. Up to four different cycles may be
used and you may adjust the time or speed of the cycle
for each. CYCLE COLORS lets you create cycle animation
and the appearance of movement. Select CYCLE COLORS
with the right mouse button. When the CYCLE COLOR MENU
requester window is on you will notice that the
currently active channel has a highlight FRAME around
the channel box. You may add one or more channels to
the currently active one by clicking the left mouse
button on the box or boxes of your choice. The buttons
of the on channels will be highlighted. If a channel
is on and you wish to turn it off do so by clicking the
left mouse button on its box. The speed of each cycle
channel may be adjusted with the CYCLE RATE slider in
the center of the window. The box with a highlight
FRAME around it will be the channel affected by any
change in the rate. Numbers will show how much you
change the rate.   The two range markers may also be
moved to change the EFFECT. If you are working with
the DEFAULT PALETTE, the one marker will be black with

small white dots. The other is white with small black dots. The cycle occurs from the color bracketed with the black marker toward the color bracketed with the white marker. You can click the left mouse button on a bracket and place it where you want. By reversing the positions of the white and black brackets you can reverse the flow of the cycle. The UNDO box undoes the last action. CYCLE turns on the cycle EFFECT. The OK box will return you to the screen to witness your image in the cycle mode and CANCEL is the way out if you change your mind. CYCLE COLORS OFF may be selected from the MENU to turn off the CYCLE COLORS EFFECT. CYCLE DRAW is a procedure for allowing the chosen brush to cycle through a chosen range of colors while you draw with the brush. The faster you move the brush the greater the space between the cycling colors. Shape selection will also alter the CYCLE DRAW option. To see the EFFECT select CYCLE COLORS. CYCLE DRAW has the same kind of requester window as CYCLE COLORS. To quit CYCLE DRAW select CYCLE DRAW OFF with the right mouse button from the MENU.

MIRRORS duplicates what you draw in one area as a MIRROR image in another area. Select MIRRORS with the right mouse button. A requester window lets you select a box for VERTICAL, HORIZONTAL or DIAGONAL MIRRORS. The MIRROR EFFECT relates to a center. The default is the center of the screen, however you may change the POINT to another area of the screen by setting the point. Move the mouse until the vertical and horizontal ghost lines are on the POINT and then click with the left mouse button. If you want to see the current position of the POINT select SHOW MIRROR POINT. A click of the left mouse button will return the MIRRORS requester. The box OK activates the option and CANCEL is if you decide not to use the MIRROR. MIRRORS OFF turns this option off.

Also under the SPECIAL MENU are commands that turn the SHAPE OPTIONS ON and SHAPE OPTIONS OFF after these options have been defined in the SHAPE OPTIONS MENU. After choosing a particular SHAPE from the SHAPES MENU you may exercise the various options of that SHAPE by selecting SHAPE OPTIONS ON with the right mouse button. The requester for each SHAPE will DISPLAY the options specific to that SHAPE. If you change from the default options you must select the LOCK box in the SHAPE OPTIONS MENU by clicking the left mouse button on the box. If you do not LOCK the settings the default settings will be active when the shape is picked. UNLOCK removes the settings. RESET puts the settings

at the default. LAST places the settings at their last
positions prior to the current alteration even if you
turned the option boxes off.   OK keeps the current
placements. CANCEL exits the MENU with no change.   The
OPT box in the FAST MENU also turns the SHAPE OPTIONS
on.   The KEYBOARD command to DISPLAY the SHAPE OPTIONS
requester is (Right AMIGA A + O).

     The   next   command under the SPECIAL heading is
EFFECTS.   To invoke EFFECTS from the KEYBOARD type
(RIGHT   AMIGA A + E).   The EFFECTS MENU contains a lot
of the magic of AEGIS IMAGES.   EFFECTS is summoned with
the   right   mouse button.   Once the EFFECTS MENU is in
view you may select any of the EFFECTS and even combine
several   with   clicks of the left mouse button on the
respective MENU boxes to highlight the EFFECTS you want
to use.   OK exits the requester. Each of the various
EFFECTS will be described in the next paragraphs to
give you some idea of their versitility.

     The first EFFECT is named PANTOGRAPH. It lets you
determine a starting POINT in an image in the middle of
an   area   that you wish to reproduce exactly in another
part of the screen, even in an area already designed.
Any   BRUSH, SHAPE or FILL when moved in the destination
area will reproduce the image at the POINT of origin.
Rapid, broken lines will reproduce a portion of the
original area or by working the entire area around the
destination POINT a complete twin of the original area
may be deposited. Choose SET SOURCE and SET
DESTINATION from the MENU. The source POINT and
destination POINT are set by clicking the left mouse
button at those points in the image. Verify the
settings by clicking the left mouse button on OK in the
PANTOGRAPH requester and again in the EFFECTS MENU
requester. Now, choose the BRUSH and SHAPE you want to
use and as you draw across the destination area the
source area will appear in direct relationship to the
two points. No transfer will occur unless you draw in
the area.

     To turn PANTOGRAPH off click the left mouse button
on its box in the EFFECTS MENU.

     UNDER may be selected from the EFFECTS MENU. In
the UNDER requester you may pick those colors in the
current PALETTE which will not be covered by any of the
other colors when you paint over the protected colors.
By clicking the left mouse button on a color you mark
it as protected. To un-mark a color click the left
mouse button on it a second time. SET marks the entire

PALETTE. INVERT will reverse the marks clearing the previously marked colors and newly marking all others. Remember that marked colors stay on top and unmarked will paint UNDER the marked colors. RANGE lets you select a RANGE of colors to mark. Click the left mouse button on the first color in the RANGE and then on another color. All between the two colors will be marked. CLEAR lets you start over. OK in this MENU enters the choices and CANCEL rejects the choices. Another OK must be clicked in the EFFECTS MENU to return to the screen and use UNDER. This is a good option to use with AIRBRUSH since it can be made to function as a frisket protecting those areas that you do not want the AIRBRUSH to spray into.

GRID can be turned on to cause shapes to begin and end or be placed on a GRID designed in the GRID requester. All the various tools except FREEHAND DRAWING will conform to the points of intersection on the GRID. You may create a GRID from 2 to 30 pixels between each LINE. You also have the options of making a HGRID (horizontal), VGRID (vertical) or both by clicking the left mouse button on both boxes. SHOW will DISPLAY the GRID. The GRID will not be visible when you return to the working screen. You can draw lines on the GRID and FRAME it and SAVE it as a WINDOW and put it on the SWAP SCREEN for recalling to the front screen or you can SHOW the GRID on top of your image on the screen. A click of the left mouse button will return the requester. Use the mouse to set the sliders in the Horz. and Vert. bars. OK accepts your GRID settings and CANCEL halts your changes. Again, OK must be selected from the EFFECTS MENU as well. The GRID may be turned off by selecting GRID in the EFFECTS MENU and picking CANCEL.

SPREAD is a function under EFFECTS that can FILL an area with a range of colors, shades of gray or a monochromatic blend. The process is called dithering and the percentage of dithering can be set from 0% to 100% with 100% being the finest appearing like an airbrush spray. The SPREAD FILLS requester lets you choose a Horz.(top to bottom), Vert. (left to right) or LINE which does a spread fill LINE by LINE. The LINE fill will stop at any shape bounded by a LINE so if you want a fine gradation as a background leave a gap in any shapes and do the background fill first, then paint the internal shapes. The RANGE markers set the first and last color of the SPREAD. Remember to click the left mouse button on the box of the first color and then click the left mouse button on the last color.

44

Adjust the % of dithering in the DITHERING bar. As usual, OK fixes the settings and CANCEL exits cancelling any changes. You need to click on OK in the EFFECTS MENU to proceed with a SPREAD FILL. Choose the FILL command from the SHAPE MENU and when you click the left mouse button on a shape bounded by a LINE or an area of solid color the area will be filled with a SPREAD. If the range you selected had only four colors then the area would be roughly divided into four equal areas of each of the four colors with adjacent colors spilling into each others space. A smooth blend of gray or a monochrome shading can be effected by creating a RANGE between a light and a dark color. Be careful if you change or include the first three colors since these are used by AEGIS IMAGES to create its menus. If you reduce the contrast in these colors the menus may disappear or be hard to read. The CIRCLE chosen from SHAPE may be used with the FILLED option to make a SPREAD FILL circle. Various SHAPES may be used in the same fashion. From time to time it is advised to switch from the FILL to the DRAW and back to FILL without drawing anything just to refresh the UNDO function so that a lot of time consuming fills would not be lost in correcting the image. These switches cause UNDO to only erase the last FILL if you so wish rather than removing every SPREAD FILL since you chose the option.

CONSTRAIN under the EFFECTS MENU can make lines conform to set angles. From the requester you can determine if the lines will be H/V (horizontal,vertical), 45 degrees and or 30/60 degrees. Any one or all of these may be used. Pick OK from this MENU and OK from the EFFECTS MENU to use CONSTRAIN or let CANCEL back you out. To leave CONSTRAIN select it from the EFFECTS MENU and click CANCEL.

If you want to make PATTERNS larger than the PATTERNS that you can create in the color PALETTE then TILE under EFFECTS is the command to use. From any screen you can use TILE to place a cursor POINT on one corner of an area by clicking the left mouse button once. Now just move the cursor to the opposite corner of the area that you are using to replicate and click the left mouse button a second time. Pick OK from the EFFECTS MENU. Choose a BRUSH and SHAPE from the TITLE MENU BAR. As you paint across the screen your chosen rectangle will be revealed as a repeating PATTERN TILE. Turn TILE off by selecting it a second time from the EFFECTS MENU.

ANTIALIAS from the EFFECTS MENU helps to smooth out jagged diagonal lines and any edges by depositing a color averaged between the current background color and the functioning foreground color. After selecting ANTIALIAS set OK in the EFFECTS MENU. Select ANTIALIAS a second time from the EFFECTS MENU to turn this option off.

Now we will explore how AEGIS IMAGES offers COLOR selection. AEGIS IMAGES uses a PALETTE of 32 colors. It lets you change the hue, saturation or value of any of these 32 colors. If you have used a color from the current PALETTE in creating an image and then change that color you will notice that all areas of that in the image will change. Be aware that AEGIS IMAGES uses the first three color boxes in the PALETTE to make the menus,etc., so any alteration of these could reduce the contrast so that the menus would be impossible to read. Changes in color will also change any PATTERNS composed of those colors.

The FAST MENU displays the current COLOR PALETTE plus the last four PATTERNS used by the program. You can use any color in the PALETTE by clicking the left mouse button on the box of your choice. A FRAME will surround the color box. To change COLOR select another box in the same fashion.

If you pull down the COLOR MENU you can select PICK COLOR by releasing the right mouse button on this option. This lets you click the left mouse button on any screen color to make it the active brush color. This is most helpful when you are having difficulty deciding the exact color. Surrounding color will affect the way a color looks and colors may look lighter, darker or of a different hue when observed in the PALETTE window adjacent to other colors.

If however, you release the right mouse button on COLORS from the COLOR MENU a COLOR EDIT requester will open. The KEYBOARD command is (Right AMIGA A + C). In the DISPLAY will be slider bars for HUE (name of a color), LUM (the value or lightness or darkness) and SAT (the relative saturation or purity of the hue). These sliders in the bars may be adjusted to any range from 0 to 255. If these are not shown, click the left mouse button on the HLS box to make changes in these bars. This box toggles between HLS and RGB. RGB, when active, produces three slider bars allowing control over the amount of red, green or blue in any color. Slider control numbers from 0 to 15 let you set precise

46

amounts to opt for any of the 4096 possible variations.

To COPY any color to another box before altering the color click the left mouse button on the color of your choice and then click the left mouse button on COPY and next on the color box which will be replaced.

If you click the left mouse button on RANGE then on the box of a color and again on another color a RANGE will be created betweeen the first and second choices.

When you can not determine the color you want to alter from the PALETTE because you can not tell, for example, which of several blues you want, simply click the left mouse button on PICK and the requester window will close so you can PICK the color from your image on the full screen by placing the cursor POINT on an area of that color and clicking the left mouse button. The COLOR EDIT requester will reopen with the color you clicked framed in the PALETTE. The KEYBOARD command is (Right AMIGA A + G).

TRANS stands for transparency and when this option is active you may paint over areas the under colors will be changed yielding an EFFECT of seeing through glass, smoke or fog. The range of selected colors for the EFFECT may be set by placing the range markers. Pick OK to make TRANS active. Pick a brush and shape to use. This will remain active until you make another selection.

GLOW is similar. When GLOW is selected from the COLOR EDIT requester you can set the range markers. Pick OK to use and select a brush and shape. GLOW alters a color painted over to the next color in the marked range. Any color outside the marked range will be changed to the first color in the marked range.

AEGIS IMAGES has an excellent command that permits you to use 16 prepared PATTERNS that perform just like solid colors when used with the various brushes and shapes. You can even EDIT a PATTERN or create your own custom PATTERN. Here's how. When you select PATTERNS from the COLOR MENU a PATTERN EDIT requester will appear. The KEYBOARD command is (Right AMIGA A + P). Displayed are the current 16 PATTERNS available for selection. A click of the left mouse button will pick a PATTERN for editing. Below the 16 boxes of PATTERNS you will see a box in the middle of the requester window. This box displays the chosen PATTERN as it

47

will be seen on the main screen. At the far left is magnified view of the same PATTERN. This box may be resized using the small square at the lower right corner. It can be reduced to one square. Other options are two squares horizontal, two squares vertical, four squares horizontal, four squares vertical, eight squares horizontal, eight squares vertical, two by two squares, two by four squares, two by eight squares, four by four squares, four by eight squares and eight by eight squares. Reducing the magnified area to one of these formats can facilitate PATTERN generation especially in simple designs like checkerboards for example. If you want to FILL a PATTERN with a solid background color to start a design just pick your color from the PALETTE at the bottom left of the window and click the left mouse button in the DISPLAY window in the center of the requester. This action will replace the PATTERN with a solid background color. Now, pick another color from the PALETTE and use it to make your PATTERN design one pixel at a time depressing the left mouse button and painting in the magnified view window. Change color the same way to add another color to the design. The SHIFT buttons reposition the design in the window one pixel a click on the direction of the arrow. To alter a PATTERN from the PALETTE offerings select one by clicking with the left mouse button on the box, then pick COPY and POINT to the box to be replaced and click the left mouse button again. You may now alter the PATTERN copied to the box. GET will bring a piece of the image screen into the PATTERN EDIT requester as a PATTERN to be used or changed. Select GET and the requester window will disappear revealing the entire image for your hunting. Put the block under the cursor over the area to GET and click the left mouse button. The requester will come back into view with the new PATTERN. PICK is the same command that is in the other requester windows. Use it to find a specific color from a screen image. As usual, OK accepts change and returns to screen; CANCEL backs out.

Changes you make in a PALETTE may be saved for use in future images. Choose SAVE AS COLORS from the PROJECT MENU, click the left mouse button in the title bar and type a NAME for the PALETTE and press the RETURN key. You might want to change directories and save to a DISK containing only PALETTEs. To use a stored PALETTE, pick OPEN COLORS from the PROJECT MENU and position the cursor on the NAME of the PALETTE you desire and click the left mouse button. CANCEL backs out without selecting a PALETTE.

The SHAPE MENU contains the tools used in making images with the various BRUSHES. Many of the SHAPES have options to alter the way they work. These SHAPE OPTIONS are selected from a requester. There is an icon at the top left that will show which SHAPE requester is being used. Each requester will have a LOCK box which will LOCK the settings if the SHAPE OPTIONS is turned on in the MENU or if the OPT button is active on the FAST MENU. UNLOCK returns to the default settings when a new SHAPE is picked. RESET puts the settings to their default positions. LAST changes the settings back to the last placement. OK accepts your changes and CANCEL returns to the screen without changing anything. These commands are the same for each SHAPE, however there are specific options for some of the SHAPES.

Pull down the SHAPE MENU and release on the icon of your choice to select a shape. This is usually done after picking a BRUSH from the BRUSH MENU.

The pencil icon is for FREEHAND DRAWING and has no options. This is the default SHAPE.

STRAIGHT LINE draws a LINE between two set points. Position the cursor at the origin of the LINE and click the left mouse button. Move the mouse after releasing the left mouse button to the other end of the LINE and click the left mouse button. These SHAPE OPTIONS may be chosen: REPEAT permits you to keep drawing with the STRAIGHT LINE once a STRAIGHT LINE has been placed on the screen. If you keep the left mouse button depressed after completing the first STRAIGHT LINE you may continue to draw. SHARE 1 uses the same origin POINT for subsequent lines. GIVE 1 uses the end POINT of each LINE for the origin POINT for the next LINE. DOTTED is listed in the window but is not functioning on version 1.1G of AEGIS IMAGES.

FILL covers an area bounded by a solid LINE or a solid area with the current color or PATTERN. From its requester you may pick SEED FILL to FILL the area under the cursor when the left mouse button is clicked. Another kind of FILL is a BOUNDARY FILL which lets you select an area as the outer limit of the FILL by clicking the left mouse button in this area. By clicking the left mouse button inside the bounded area you can FILL all the different areas inside the boundary.

49

A click of the right mouse button will stop and cancel an action in AEGIS IMAGES during the action.

RECTANGLE will draw a RECTANGLE from a POINT where you place the cursor and click the left mouse button, release it and move the mouse to the location of the opposite corner and click the left mouse button again. A second option is to pick CEN. & CORNER instead of DIAG. CORNERS. Using the second option, put the cursor at the center of the rectangle and click the left mouse button. Now, move the cursor to one of the corners to form the rectangle and click the left mouse button again. SHAPE OPTIONS are FILLED which gives a solid RECTANGLE, REPEAT, SHARE 1 and GIVE 1. The last three are defined above.

CIRCLE will make circles from a CENTER if you choose this method and place the cursor where the CENTER of the CIRCLE will be and click the left mouse button. A ghost CIRCLE will appear which responds to movement of the mouse allowing you to size the CIRCLE and finish by clicking the left mouse button. To make a CIRCLE using DIAMETER, put the cursor where the side of the CIRCLE will be and click the left mouse button. Now move the cursor to the opposite side of the CIRCLE and click the left mouse button again. CIRCUMFERENCE makes a CIRCLE if you place the cursor on a POINT which will be on the circumference of the CIRCLE. Next, move to another POINT on the circumference and click the left mouse button another time. Finally, move the cursor to a third POINT on the circumference and click the left mouse button and a CIRCLE will form on these three points. Other SHAPE OPTIONS are FILLED, REPEAT, SHARE 1 and GIVE 1.

POINT prints one stamp of the current brush in the current color with a click of the left mouse button. It has the SHAPE OPTION: REPEAT which is useful to draw dotted or broken lines.

POLYGON has many options so that you can select from a sub-menu from 2 to 19 sides for a POLYGON. Simply release the right mouse button on the number of sides you want. Put the cursor where the center of the POLYGON is to be and click the left mouse button. If you move the mouse you can size the POLYGON and by rotating the mouse you can adjust the position of the POLYGON on the screen.

50

PARALLELOGRAMS are made by placing the cursor on a
corner of the projected PARALLELOGRAM and then clicking
the left mouse button. Movement of the mouse will make
the first side of the shape. To stop sizing, click the
left mouse button. Now move the cursor again and the
other side of the PARALLELOGRAM will form and can be
sized. When the shape you desire is formed, click the
left mouse button again. These shapes may use these
SHAPE OPTIONS: FILLED, REPEAT, SHARE 1 and GIVE 2.
GIVE 2 lets the last two points of one shape become the
first two points of the next shape.

TRIANGLES may be drawn by first placing the cursor
on the first corner of a projected TRIANGLE and
clicking the left mouse button, then moving the cursor
to the next corner and clicking the left mouse button
again, and, lastly, by moving the cursor to the last
corner of the TRIANGLE and clicking the left mouse
button. TRIANGLES have the following SHAPE OPTIONS:
FILLED, REPEAT, SHARE 1, SHARE 2, GIVE 1 and GIVE 2.
SHARE 2 uses the last two corners of a TRIANGLE to set
the first two corners of the next TRIANGLE.

ELLIPSES are designed by setting three points.
The first two points set the long axis of the ELLIPSE.
Choose POINT one and click the left mouse button. Move
the cursor to POINT two and click the left mouse
button. Movement of the cursor now will size the
ELLIPSE and turn it in different positions. Click the
left mouse button when you are satisfied with the
design of the ELLIPSE. ELLIPSES have these SHAPE
OPTIONS: FILLED, REPEAT, SHARE 1, SHARE 2, GIVE 2 and
GIVE 1.

ARCS are drawn by either selecting ENDS & CEN
which stands for ends and center or picking 3 PNTS ON
ARC which stands for three points on the arc. If you
choose the ENDS & CEN you place the cursor at the
center POINT and click the left mouse button. Next,
move the cursor to the end of the ARC and click the
left mouse button. Now, move the cursor to the other
end of the ARC and when you have it right click the
left mouse button. To use 3 PNTS ON ARC place the
cursor at one end of the ARC and click the left mouse
button. Next, go to the other end of the ARC and click
the left mouse button again. Now, move the cursor to a
POINT on the ARC to form the ARC and when it is the way
you want it to be, click the left mouse button. SHAPE
OPTIONS for ARCS include: REPEAT, FILLED, WEDGE, SHARE
1, SHARE 2, GIVE 1 and GIVE 2.

51

CURVES may be made in two ways. One way is SEQ PNTS which means sequential points. First, put the cursor on the first end of the CURVE and click the left mouse button. Second, move the cursor to the highest POINT of the CURVE and click the left mouse button. Third, move the cursor to the other end of the CURVE and click the left mouse button. Another method is the ENDS THEN CEN which employs two ends and a center point. First put the cursor on the first end of the CURVE and click the left mouse button. Second, move the cursor to the opposite end and click the left mouse button. Third, move the cursor around to design the CURVE and, when what you see is what you want, click the left mouse button. CURVES offer these SHAPE OPTIONS: REPEAT, SHARE 1, SHARE 2, GIVE 1 and GIVE 2.

The ERASE command is opened from the SHAPE MENU. Release the right mouse button on ERASE. ERASE uses the current brush and background color and by depressing the left mouse button you can draw with the background color erasing the area under the cursor. ERASE stops when you pick another SHAPE and reverts back to the last active color.

AEGIS IMAGES has a limited number of FONTS in the TEXT option which may be used to type in letters on top of your screen image or in spaces reserved for TEXT. The current color will be the color of the letters. Choose the FONTS first by releasing the right mouse button on FONTS. The KEYBOARD command for FONTS is (Right AMIGA A + F). The FONTS requester will NAME the available FONTS and the current selection will be displayed. Click the left mouse button on the FONT of your choice. Pick OK to use or CANCEL to exit with no change.

Select TEXT from the SHAPE MENU by releasing the right mouse button on TEXT. Position the cursor on the screen where the TEXT will begin. The TEXT cursor shows the top of the capital letters, the top of the lower case and the bottom of the decenders for letters like p and y. Type your letters from the KEYBOARD. Use the BACK SPACE to ERASE and use the RETURN key to drop down one LINE and begin under the first letter in the LINE above.

AEGIS IMAGES has 20 BRUSHES for use in the program and 16 of these BRUSHES may be changed to customize them to your specific needs. Release the right mouse button on BRUSH and on the icon of the BRUSH POINT you wish to use. Next select the SHAPE tool from its MENU

and the COLOR from its respective MENU. Now, you are
ready to make your mark by depressing the left mouse
button while moving the mouse cursor.
    To customize a BRUSH release the right mouse
button on BRUSHES at the bottom of the BRUSH MENU. A
BRUSH EDIT MENU will open. The 16 availabe BRUSHES
will be presented at the top of this window. Click the
left mouse button on the icon of the BRUSH that you
want to change. A magnified version of that BRUSH will
appear in the large rectangle on the left side. In the
center of the window a rectangle shows the actual size
of the BRUSH on the screen. Between these boxes is a
shift button which moves the DISPLAY according to which
arrow you click with the left mouse button. To EDIT
the BRUSH you add or take away pixels with the tools at
the bottom of this MENU. ERASE shows a pencil with an
eraser turned down. A click on this icon activates it
and if you put the cursor in the magnified view you can
remove pixels by clicking the left mouse button. If
you depress the left mouse button you can remove pixels
continuously. Likewise, if you click the left mouse
button on the icon with a pencil point turned down this
box will be active and any click of the left mouse
button will add pixel points under the cursor.
Depressing the left mouse button and moving the cursor
will draw. Between the pencil icons is a FILL box. If
the ERASE box is highlighted, a click on FILL will FILL
the magnified view with blanks. If, however, the DRAW
box is highlighted, a click on FILL will deposit pixels
over the area of the magnified view. If you want to
keep a BRUSH for use and also have an altered version
of that BRUSH then use COPY and select the BRUSH by
clicking the left mouse button on the icon of the BRUSH
you want to EDIT, click the same button on COPY and
then on the BRUSH you are replacing with this COPY.
Now, use the pencils to EDIT the COPY. GET will
capture any area from the screen for use as a BRUSH.
The background color will be transparent and all other
colors will be picked up as though they were one color.
When you click the left mouse button on GET, the
requester window will disappear and a FRAME will be on
the screen indicating the area of the BRUSH capture.
Press the left mouse button to pick up the captured
BRUSH. At the bottom of the BRUSH EDIT MENU are the
usual OK to use box and CANCEL to exit boxes.

    AEGIS IMAGES has a fine AIRBRUSH function located
under the BRUSH MENU. Select AIRBRUSH by releasing the
right mouse button on AIRBRUSH. A requester will
appear containing a slider control for SPRAY (the
number of pixels in the spray) and SPREAD (the size of

the area covered by the spray). By moving the cursor in the slider bar you can raise of lower the levels. The DISPLAY box shows the spray pattern as actual screen size. Click the left mouse button on OK to begin using the AIRBRUSH or CANCEL to exit. The AIRBRUSH will spray with whatever SHAPE tool was active when AIRBRUSH is selected. The PENCIL icon is a good choice. The current PALETTE color will be the spray paint. Move the cursor while depressing the left mouse button to spray the AIRBRUSH. Use UNDER from the EFFECTS MENU to create stencils and friskets for use with the AIRBRUSH. Protected colors will not be sprayed on. Subtle modelling can be achieved using the AIRBRUSH.

The following is a review of the KEYBOARD commands available for AEGIS IMAGES:

```
(Right AMIGA A + C) = COLOR EDIT
(Right AMIGA A + E) = EFFECTS
(Right AMIGA A + F) = FONTS
(Right AMIGA A + G) = GET COLOR FROM SCREEN
(Right AMIGA A + K) = MAGNIFY
(Right AMIGA A + M) = Returns IMAGES to front
(Right AMIGA A + N) = WORKBENCH/CLI to front
(Right AMIGA A + O) = SHAPE OPTIONS
(Right AMIGA A + P) = PATTERN EDIT
(Right AMIGA A + Q) = EXITS AEGIS IMAGES
(Right AMIGA A + S) = SWAPS SCREENS
(Right AMIGA A + V) = UNDO
(Right AMIGA A + Z) = CLEARS SCREEN
```

This concludes a description of the many commands waiting for your selection in AEGIS IMAGES.

CHAPTER SIX

USING AEGIS ANIMATOR

AEGIS ANIMATOR is a program for putting together animations created from backgrounds and multi-colored objects created with AEGIS IMAGES or any of the other IFF format paint programs listed in the previous chapters. A background is a full screen image saved to DISK with the designation (.pic) added at the end of its name. Backgrounds are like stage sets on which the movement takes place. OBJECTS are images saved to DISK with (.win) added to the end of their names. In AEGIS ANIMATOR you can change the size of the OBJECT, alter the color and move them around the screen in front of the background. Up to nine different scripts can be put together, rearranged and timed on a storyboard to create videos and slide shows. In addition to the multi-colored OBJECTS, AEGIS ANIMATOR can make solid color polygons which change shape, size, position, as well as rotate around x, y and z axis. Especially fine is the ability to draw a beginning shape and an end shape and have the computer morph or FILL in the transformation in time from one shape to the other.

To LOAD the program, insert the AEGIS ANIMATOR DISK after the KICKSTART 1.1 DISK boots the system. Click the left mouse button on the icons to open the program. If you have worked through the paint programs you should be aware of the selection and use of the command functions from the MENU BAR. I will not describe the operations in as much detail as in the other chapters. AEGIS ANIMATOR has the following MENU items:

PROJECT:

UNDO = Reverts back to the screen before the last command.

FAST MENU = Makes this MENU appear or disappear.

NEW SCRIPT = Deletes the current script and opens a new one.

STORAGE = Opens the storage requester.

STORYBOARD = Opens the storyboard window.

COLOR = Opens the color requester.

TIME = Opens the time requester.

STATUS = Shows the available memory in the MENU BAR.

EXIT = Exits the program.

CREATE:

LINE = Makes a single LINE OBJECT .

POLYGON FILLED = Makes a solid shape like stretching a rubber band around a shape.

POLYGON OUTLINE = Makes an outline like stretching a rubber band around a shape.

CIRCLE FILLED = Makes a solid circle of 16 points.

CIRCLE OUTLINE = Makes an outline of a circle.

STAR FILLED = Makes a solid 5 pointed star.

STAR OUTLINE = Makes an outline of a 5 pointed star.

BLOCK = Makes a four sided mask OBJECT .

CLONE = Copies OBJECTS.

DESTROY = Deletes an OBJECT in the present and future if it is part of an animation.

MOVE:

MOVE SIDEWAYS = Moves an OBJECT .

MOVE IN = Moves OBJECTS back in successive planes allowing some to be in front of others.

MOVE OUT = Moves OBJECTS forward in successive planes allowing some to be in front of others.

ROTATE IN PLANE = Rotates an OBJECT around a center point.

ROTATE AROUND X = Rotates an OBJECT around an x axis (horizontal line).

ROTATE AROUND Y = Rotates an OBJECT around a y axis (vertical line).

SIZE = Enlarges or reduces an OBJECT at a selected point.

PATH = Sets a path of movement for an OBJECT to follow.

CHANGE COLOR = Makes the current color the color of the current color at the start of the tween.

CHANGE TYPE = Shifts between filled and outline shapes.

MORPH LOOP = Makes a new shape by moving the points composing the OBJECT .

MORPH HOOK = Makes a new shape by moving, adding or deleting points composing the OBJECT .

SELECT

POINT = Makes the current selection affect one point.

POINTS = Makes the current selection affect many points.

SEGMENT = Makes the current selection affect a segment of an OBJECT .

POLYGON = Makes the current selection an OBJECT .

POLYGONS = Makes the current selection a number of OBJECTS.

ALL = Picks all OBJECTS in the animation for a command.

TIME:

NEXT TWEEN = Goes to the next tween or if there are no more tweens creates a new one.

57

REPLAY TWEEN = Plays the current tween again.

REPLAY ALL = Plays the current animation again.

PLAY LOOP = Plays an animation over and over until stopped.

GHOST MODE = Displays OBJECTS as outline.

SEE TWEEN AT END = In editing, all tweens will be shown at the end.

SEE TWEEN AT BEGIN = In editing, all tweens will be shown at the beginning.

COLOR:

Opens the COLOR PALETTE highlighting the current color. Select new colors from this PALETTE.

STORYBOARD:

PROJECT GO INTO = Sets EDIT mode in the current window.

PROJECT SPEED = Opens the time requester.

PROJECT ABOUT ANI = Gives information about the program.

PROJECT STATUS = Shows available memory in the MENU BAR.

PROJECT EXIT = Exits the program.

EDIT SPLICE = Copies the current tween and future tweens into another window.

EDIT CUT = Cuts the current tween and future tweens into another window.

EDIT DELETE = Deletes all animation from the current window.

EDIT ACTIVATE = Same as PLAY LOOP in the current window.

AEGIS ANIMATOR presents a FAST MENU on its screen which permits you to select icons for every function of the MENU BAR. The first icon is POINT. Moving from top left to bottom right the other icons are: POINTS, SEGMENT POLYGON, POLYGONS, ALL, STATUS (gauge), HELP (?), FUNCTION, UNDO, MOVE SIDEWAYS (hand), MOVE IN, OUT (OUT), PATH (curved line), SIZE (four arrows), ROTATE (curve with arrow), MORPH LOOP (noose), STORAGE (disk), STORYBOARD (9 tiles), COLOR requester (PALETTE), TIME requester (Time), POLYGON CREATE (pointer), CHANGE COLOR (brush), CLONE (4 triangles), DESTROY (circle + diagonal), MORPH HOOK (hook), EXIT, PLAY LOOP (large reel), PLAY TWEEN (small reel) and ADVANCE TWEEN (camera). COLOR may be picked from the bar at the bottom.

With this basic understanding of the functions you may explore the world of animation using AEGIS ANIMATOR.

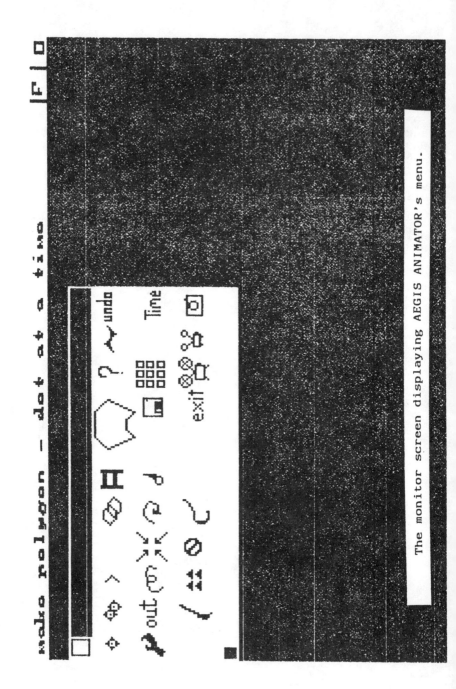

The monitor screen displaying AEGIS ANIMATOR's menu.

CHAPTER SEVEN

USING DIGI-PAINT

DIGI-PAINT by NEW TEK is a HAM (hold-and modify mode) paint program. The HAM mode allows all 4096 variations of hue, value and saturation of colors in the palette to be on the screen at the same time. Pictures digitized in the HAM mode cannot be altered in any of the other paint programs described in the previous chapters. However, images made with these programs may be edited with DIGI-PAINT. Once reworked by DIGI-PAINT, the image cannot be returned to the other programs.

The COLOR PALETTE requester for DIGI-PAINT also has 32 colors but it has sliders with which you can select any of the 4096 variations. This requester is different in that the color you create using the sliders is not one of the 32 palette colors. For example, you could have 32 tints and shades of blue in the PALETTE and make an orange color with the sliders and use this orange color to paint in you picture without altering any of the 32 blues. DIGI-PAINT is useful in editing any images saved in the IFF format and has its own set of brush points, tools and functions which are related to those of the other programs.

abcdefghijkl
mnopqrstuv
wxyz

An alphabet designed on the computer.

62

CHAPTER EIGHT

USING DIGI-VIEW

DIGI-VIEW is a program developed by New Tek for digitizing images with a video camera so that the images appear in LO-RES 32 colors or black and white HI-RES on the MONITOR screen. Another option is the 4096 color HAM mode. The DIGI-VIEW box must be plugged into the PARALLEL PORT on the back of the computer. A black and white video camera is used either on a copy stand or on a tripod for stability. Lights should be placed evenly at a 45 degree angle. If you are using the computer MONITOR to focus the image to be digitized, plug the cable from the video camera into the VIDEO-IN port on the back of the MONITOR just under the AUDIO port. Pull down the horizontal door covering the control panel on the front of the MONITOR by placing your finger in the slot under the AMIGA checkmark. At the far right of the control panel you will see VIDEO MODE. Flip the switch over to the left to the mark lettered COMP. for COMPOSITE. Take the lens cap off the video camera lens, turn on the camera by pressing the on/off button on the back of the camera or wherever the on/off switch is on the camera you are using and turn the focusing ring on the lens barrel to bring the MONITOR image into focus.

You can digitize your picture once the image to be copied is placed and focused by switching from COMP. to RGB on the VIDEO MODE control on the front of the MONITOR in the control panel and by switching the camera cable from the MONITOR back to the DIGI-VIEW box attached to the PARALLEL PORT on the computer. To avoid this switching back and forth a "Y" cable could connect the camera to both the MONITOR and the Digi-View box.

The DIGI-VIEW software DISK is inserted after KICKSTART and WORKBENCH are loaded. Open the DIGI-VIEW DISK icon by clicking the left mouse button twice. In the window that opens, you will observe two tool icons. The RGB icon is for LO-RES 32 color images and the HIRES icon is for HI-RES black and white images. If you wish to digitize in LO-RES color, click the left mouse button twice on the RGB icon. In a few seconds a MENU BAR will be in view at the top of the screen revealing five items whenever the right mouse button is depressed. These menu items are selected by highlighting them and then releasing the right mouse button.

When you are ready to digitize, rotate the color filter wheel under the video camera lens so that the red segment is directly under the camera lens. Select the RED menu option with the right mouse button and release on DIGITIZE. The image under the video camera will be scanned and turned into a digitized format which can be reassembled into a picture by the computer. This digitized signal may even be sent over telephone lines to a remote computer. The scanning takes about ten seconds for each of the three filters. Once the RED is digitized, the program will automatically adjust the BRIGHTNESS and CONTRAST. It will do this after each color is scanned. The next step is to rotate the color wheel to line up the GREEN wedge under the lens. Repeat the same process for GREEN as you did for RED. Again, rotate the color wheel to line up the BLUE wedge under the lens and repeat the process as you did earlier for RED each time choosing the same color from the menu as the wedge. Now, depress the right mouse button and release on CONTROLS. This will DISPLAY a control panel with vertical slider bars to adjust the Bri (brightness), Con (contrast), Sat (saturation), Blu (to add blue, move the slider marker higher; to add more yellow, move the slider marker lower), Red (to add red move the slider marker higher; to add green move the slider marker lower), Sharp (sharpness may be raised to increase sharpness but increases the grain and when its marker is lower it smoothes out the grain into broad areas of tone like a posterization). DEFAULT sets all sliders to the CENTER positions. OK removes the control panel without making any changes. Once you have adjusted the CONTROLS and you want to sample the effect of your changes you may click the left mouse button on the 4096 box to see the digitized image in full color HAM mode. If you prefer, you may select the 32 box to see the image in the LO-RES 32 color mode. To halt either the digitization or the replay of the DISPLAY, simply click the left mouse button during the action.

Images may be saved to a storage DISK by naming the DISK drive as the destination. For example, type: (DF1:LO-RES/NAME) in the window of the SAVE requester. Do not type the brackets. NAME, of couse, is any NAME you give one of your images that has been digitized. Under the PROJECT menu are the following options: SAVE IFF, SAVE RGB, LOAD RGB, CALIBRATE and QUIT. If you pick SAVE IFF you can release on 4096 COLOR to save a HAM image. HAM images may be edited with the

DIGI-PAINT program. 32 COLOR will save an IFF image. These may be changed with any of the IFF compatible paint programs described in this book. B/W (Red) saves an IFF image as a black and white image. SAVE RGB saves the separations for editing at a future time. LOAD RGB loads a saved RGB FILE for editing with the control panel. Under CALIBRATE, select SYNC to use a video camera that is not RS-170 compatible but does have a 2:1 interlace. WIDTH adjusts the proportions of the digitized picture.

HIRES has only two menu options: PROJECT and HI-RES. Select HI-RES and release on DIGITIZE and a HI-RES, black and white image composed of as many as 16 variations of value (white to black) will appear in about 20 seconds. CONTROLS has Bri (brightness), Con (contrast) and Sharp (sharpness) controls to fine tune the black and white picture.

With this program you can place anything in front of the lens of the video camera and prepare an image for additional work with the paint programs. Photographs, drawings, paintings, illustrations, lettering, projected slides, still video or anything that is not moving (unless you want blurred forms) may be captured to DISK. You can even digitize a portrait if your model is able to sit absolutely motionless for about 30 seconds. Any movement will result in unmodified primary colors appearing along the edges of shapes. If you like this kind of special effect, try having your subject move slightly or move your picture during each of the three separations. This is truly a fine program expanding the possibilities of creating art, videos and animations with a computer.

PLAINSONG

Graphic designs made with the computer.

CHAPTER NINE

USING GENLOCK AND VIDEO

The Commodore AMIGA GENLOCK 1300 is a hardware
device that is able to combine computer graphics, audio
and animation with a video signal creating a new
picture which may be displayed on the MONITOR and taped
on videotape. The external video source may be a video
camera, videotape player, a VCR or a laser disc. The
GENLOCK substitutes the Amiga's background color (color
0) in any computer graphic image with the picture from
the external video source. If, for example, your
background color was black, then all other colors used
to make the image would overlay the black. These black
areas (color 0) of the screen would DISPLAY the video
signal as a picture running in the background areas.
One example is a rectangular FRAME filled with the
background color in a computer design. That portion of
the video image occupying the same location as the
rectangle would be displayed in the area of the
rectangle surrounded by the computer design. This
composite picture can be seen on the MONITOR and stored
by videotapimg. If you are running a videotape on a
VCR you will need another VCR to record.

Digitized pictures and lettering from character
generators may also be added to videos using this
system.

The GENLOCK attaches to the RGB (red,green and
blue) port of the computer. The RGB signal is combined
with the input from the VIDEO IN port. This
combination is sent to the RGB-OUT port and the
COMPOSITE VIDEO-OUT port. Switches on GENLOCK let you
set up these options.

Remember, to record to videotape you will need two
VCR's or a VCR and a videotape player. Hook up the
VCR's VIDEO-IN port to the COMPOSITE VIDEO port on the
back of the computer (NOT the MONITOR) with a
double-ended RCA jack. Stereo sound can be hooked up
with cables to the computer to add recorded music,
digitized sound or voice over. When you are ready to
record, press the RECORD button on the VCR.

Many layers of images may be combined by
overlapping computer graphics on video, videotaping and
designing additional computer art to place on top of a
video prior to further taping. Be advised that GENLOCK

67

only allows video to run in the background. You cannot create computer backgrounds with this program and have video images moving on top of the computer generated background.

CHAPTER TEN

USING SLIDESHOW

The SLIDESHOW program displays individual still pictures saved to DISK from paint programs like DeluxePaint and Aegis Images. GraphiCraft images must be loaded into DeluxePaint, renamed and saved as a DeluxePaint file.

SLIDESHOW lets you select the pictures to be shown in succession. You determine the length of time that each image stays on the screen and any special effects associated with presenting and changing each "slide".

To make a slide show you will need a copy of the SLIDESHOW program which is in the public domain. Copy the SLIDESHOW program to the same disk containing your images. RENAME this DISK: SLIDESHOW. Place it in the external DISK drive and put WORKBENCH in the internal DISK drive.

Next, OPEN the CLI (Command Line Interpreter) from the WORKBENCH window. If you do not see its icon in the WORKBENCH window look in the SYSTEM drawer. At the 1> prompt type: CD DF1: and press the RETURN key. Next type: ED FROM SCRIPT and then press the RETURN key. This will open an ED FILE named SCRIPT. In this FILE type your commands for your SCRIPT.

Press the (ESC) key + (T) to move the cursor to the top of the FILE. (ESC) + (D) will delete the current line. (ESC) + (B) moves to the bottom of the file. To change existing text, type the new text and then delete the old text. The names must be exactly the same as the names you gave your pictures. Press the RETURN key at the end of each line. If you do not follow this correctly the show will not run. The following is a sample of a SCRIPT COMMAND FILE. The words in the brackets are NOT typed in the command file and are here only to explain each line.

flip pointer   (flips the pointer to be put offscreen)
load one   (loads the first picture-use your name)
darken   (darkens screen)
pulldn (pulls the image down)
cycle on (turns on the cycle command for cycle images)
wait 2 (delays the next image by the number used)
load two (loads the next picture- again, use your name)

69

This SCRIPT COMMAND FILE may continue to load images until the disk is filled. Other options include:

show (which presents the slide fast)
scrollup (screen image moves up as next image
          appears)
rolldn (rolls screen image down)
pulldn (pulls next image down over last image)
fade in (new image fades in- time may be added)
fade out (current image fades out- time may be added)
fade in time 6
fade out time 4
rollup (new image rolls up over last image)
fade out quick (screen image disappears fast)
cycle on next (cycle next image)
cycle on current (cycle current image)
restore current (restores current image)
restart (loop through all images)

When you finish creating your SCRIPT COMMAND FILE, press the (ESC) key and then the (x) key to save your file named "SCRIPT." (ESC) + (Q) exits the editing without saving the file.

CAUTION: Do a "warm boot" before running SLIDESHOW if you are showing HI-RES images one after another to insure that the computer has enough memory to present the show.

To run the SLIDESHOW program, place the WORKBENCH DISK in drive DF0: and your SLIDESHOW DISK in the external drive DF1:.

Type CD DF1: and press RETURN.
Type SLIDESHOW SCRIPT and press RETURN.

The SLIDESHOW program and your images will LOAD. If you included a restart line SCRIPT will loop continuously through the COMMAND FILE showing the images as you directed. If the program fails to LOAD check the COMMAND FILE for wrong names. If your images are in DRAWERS include the path after load in your COMMAND FILE. The (esc) key brings the WORKBENCH screen to the front allowing you to exit SLIDESHOW.

Use this page to make notes for your SCRIPT.

(Remember that you must use the exact same names as you named your images and that the SLIDESHOW, SCRIPT and your images must all be in the same directory.)

CHAPTER ELEVEN

USING DELUXE VIDEO CONSTRUCTION SET

The DELUXE VIDEO CONSTRUCTION SET by Electronic Arts is a program for creating animated videos using images created with IFF paint programs and digitized images saved to DISK in the IFF format as backgrounds. On these backgrounds you may make OBJECTS created with the paint programs MOVE around and change size. In addition, many different EFFECTS may be performed on the backgrounds and the OBJECTS such as FADE IN and FADE OUT. music, digitized sound, lettering and a library of POLYGON shapes may also be mixed into the production. All these scenes can be organized into a VIDEO SCRIPT and may be viewed on a MONITOR or ported out to a VCR for videotaping. This is a powerful tool for video programming and has numerous special EFFECTS which may be combined in so many different ways that a full description of every function would require a book by itself. This chapter will present the program to you and help you get started. Experiment with the EFFECTS and timing and record the results. For serious application, it is advisable to design a worksheet outlining the things you want to do and how they are to be accomplished, relating the various scenes and EFFECTS. Do not get discouraged. This program is complicated; but the results can be very professional and in time you will become familiar with the possibilities.

DELUXE VIDEO CONSTRUCTION SET uses these DISKs:

DVIDEO is the MASTER KEY DISK.

MAKER is an unprotected DISK for making videos and has drawers for PICTURES, OBJECTS, SOUNDS, MUSIC and INSTRUMENTS.

PARTS and UTILITIES has PICTURES, OBJECTS, SOUNDS, MUSIC and INSTRUMENTS which can be used in videos. It also has FRAMER for making animations and VIDCHECK to compress videos so that they take up less DISK storage space and UNPACK to cut parts from one video and put the parts in another or place the cut parts in storage. Several paint programs like DELUXEPAINT and AEGIS IMAGES use the same file format (IFF) as DELUXE VIDEO CONSTRUCTION SET. Backgrounds, pictures and OBJECTS may be created with these paint programs and saved on the PARTS and UTILITIES DISK in the PICTURES and

OBJECTS drawers by inserting this DISK <u>instead</u> of a storage DISK with drawers for LO-RES and brushes as used by DELUXEPAINT. MUSIC may be added to videos by copying instruments to the INSTRUMENTS drawer on PARTS and UTILITIES. Software programs like INSTANT MUSIC and DELUXE MUSIC CONSTRUCTION SET may be used to create the MUSIC.

PLAYER is an unprotected DISK for playing videos you create and save to this DISK.

Before you begin to work with DELUXE VIDEO CONSTRUCTION SET you will need to get at least six new 3.5 DS DD microdisks. Make your own copies of DVIDEO, MAKER, and PARTS and UTILITIES from the master disks. Next, make a working copy of the PARTS and UTILITIES DISK and RENAME as PARTS. Delete the following drawers: FRAMES, VIDCHECK and UNPACK so that you will have more room for storage. Pictures, OBJECTS, music, sounds and instruments may be stored on this DISK from other software that uses IFF format.

Now, make a working copy of MAKER. After a "warm boot" (CTRL, LEFT AMIGA and RIGHT AMIGA keys pressed at the same time) insert MAKER and EMPTY the following drawers: PICTURES, OBJECTS, SOUNDS, MUSIC and INSTRUMENTS of all files by dragging the icons to the TRASHCAN one at a time, and then clicking on the TRASHCAN icon and select EMPTY from the menu. RENAME this storage disk PLAYER.

To make an extra storage DISK with maximum storage exclude WORKBENCH on a copy of a storage DISK. To do this you initialize a new blank DISK. Copy data from your PLAYER DISK by dragging the icons of VIDEOS, PICTURES, OBJECTS, SOUNDS, MUSIC and INSTRUMENTS onto this new DISK. Now, you are ready for production of your first video.

Follow this procedure to make a video:

Insert the KICKSTART DISK at the MONITOR request. Remove KICKSTART and insert MAKER DISK at the MONITOR request for WORKBENCH. WORKBENCH is on the MAKER DISK so you do not have to LOAD a separate WORKBENCH DISK. Double-click the left mouse button on the MAKER DISK icon and double-click the left mouse button on the DVIDEO icon. A system request message will appear asking you to insert the DVIDEO MASTER KEY DISK which verifies the MAKER DISK. Re-insert the MAKER DISK at

the system request which appears on the screen.   After
this verification process, do not use the DVIDEO unless
the system requests this DISK. Use your working copies
of MAKER, PLAYER, PARTS and PARTS and UTILITIES to make
your videos.

   The Electronic Arts logo will   show   for   a   few
moments on the screen and then the VIDEO SCRIPT window
will appear. Let's look at this screen.   There   is   a
vertical   gauge on the left with an F for FULL and an E
for EMPTY. A horizontal box (left) with a yellow and a
white   vertical   division   is   called   a   SCRIPT.   A
horizontal box (right) with a yellow and a white
horizontal   division   is   called   an   EFFECT.   Time in
seconds is displayed on the dark blue TIME bar. A MENU
BAR   is   on   the   top   of   the   screen   where   it reads
DeluxeVideo. The menu headings are: PROJECT, EDIT,
SCENES,   PARTS   and   OPTIONS.   These may be selected by
placing the red arrow on the MENU BAR and picking   the
title   of   the   heading   while pressing the right mouse
button. Look at each heading to   see   the   choices   it
contains   by   keeping   the   right   mouse button pressed
while moving the red arrow down from the heading.   For
now,   use   this procedure to select PROJECT and drag to
select NEW before releasing the right mouse button.   In
the   VIDEO SCRIPT window one TRACK labelled VIDEO is in
place. Also in place is the VIDEO TRACK which has   an
EFFECT   box named SCENE which has two POINTERS touching
the horizontal line extending   from   the   VIDEO   TRACK.
These   points show the starting time and ending time of
the SCENE. The TIME is displayed. At   the   far   right
edge   and   the   bottom edge are scroll bars which allow
you to MOVE through your VIDEO SCRIPT.

   On screen is a large gray area with an EFFECT   box
named   SCENE.   Double click on this SCENE box with the
left mouse button to open the SCENE SCRIPT window. Now
you   will   have two overlapping windows: a VIDEO SCRIPT
and a SCENE SCRIPT. In the SCENE SCRIPT window, place
the   red   arrow   on the SCRIPT box and depress the left
mouse button as you drag this box down into   the   light
gray   vertical   area.   Be   sure to leave a space above
this box in the light gray area   slightly   larger   than
the   SCRIPT   box.   Release   the   left mouse button. A
window will appear asking you   what kind of   track   you
want to add. Select PICTURE with one click of the left
mouse button. A PICTURE REQUESTER will   come   up.   If
you   are   using a one DISK drive system, take the MAKER
DISK out at this point and insert a PARTS DISK. If you
are   using   a two DISK drive system, place PARTS in the

external drive and pick DF1: by clicking once with the left mouse button on its box in the DISPLAY. The ON DISK window will show the names of pictures that you have saved on the DISK. To choose a picture click once on the left mouse button while the red pointer is on theNAMEof your picture. (For a one-drive system, System Request will now ask you to insert MAKER DISK to replace PARTS DISK. Next, swap PARTS for MAKER. Again,swap MAKER for PARTS.) If you are using a two-drive system this swapping will not be necessary. Now your picture's NAME will be shown in the IN VIDEO window. To view this picture, click once with the left mouse button on the MONITOR icon. Your picture should be visible. To return to the SCENE SCRIPT, place the pointer on the BACK TO FRONT box at the upper right of the screen and click once on the left mouse button. To select this picture, click once on the left mouse button while the pointer is on the SELECT box and the NAME of your picture will MOVE to the SCRIPT box. Place the pointer on the EFFECTS box and depress the left mouse button and drag this EFFECTS box to place it so that it is in the darker gray window with the yellow point of the EFFECTS box touching the blue horizontal line. A REQUEST window is displayed. Select the LOAD box with one click of the left mouse button. When the LOAD EFFECT requester comes up, select the CUT box with one click of the left mouse button. Now, go to the MENU BAR and from the PROJECT heading pick PLAY SCENE by depressing the right mouse button until this item is highlighted; then release the right mouse button to see your picture.

In the lower right corner is a REMOTE CONTROL BOX. At the bottom of this box is a DISPLAY of seconds on the left side of the colon and jiffies or 1/60 seconds on the right of the colon. This will play for twenty seconds and stop. To return to SCENE SCRIPT, point the cursor finger on the dot in the CLOSE box on the left top of the REMOTE CONTROL BOX and click the left mouse button. This can be done even before the time is up. This REMOTE CONTROL BOX can be moved by depressing the left mouse button while the finger is on the DRAG BAR. Later, when you have made a video, this REMOTE CONTROL BOX can be used to play in reverse, forward, stop, fast reverse, fast forward, rewind, skip forward, skip reverse, single stop, restart and mute. It is designed to resemble the remote control for a VCR. You can make it disappear from view by using the FRONT-TO-BACK gadget.

Now you can add a FOREGROUND OBJECT to your video.
These images are portions of a screen like BRUSHES in
DELUXEPAINT or a .win in AEGIS IMAGES. First, pull
down a new TRACK while in the SCENE SCRIPT and place it
under the first TRACK. Select OBJECT and the OBJECT
requester will open. A list of stored OBJECTS will be
offered in the ON DISK window (if you have saved the
images and stored them in the OBJECTS drawer). Click
the left mouse button on the NAME of the OBJECT that
you wish to use in your video SCENE. The OBJECT will
be loaded into memory. Click on the TV icon to see the
OBJECT on top of the previously selected BACKGROUND.
To return to the OBJECT requester, click the FRONT-TO-
BACK gadget. Click SELECT to return to the SCENE
SCRIPT and verify the NAME of your new TRACK (look to
see if its NAME appears as a TRACK).

An OBJECT in a SCENE SCRIPT may have the following
EFFECTS:

FETCH = Preloads an OBJECT into memory to avoid a
delay in the video.

APPEAR = Determines where and when an OBJECT
will appear.

DISAPP = Causes the OBJECT to disappear at a
specific point in time.

MOVETO = Moves an OBJECT from a current position
on the background to another position over a
determined amount of time.

STAMP = Use STAMP to place an OBJECT on the
BACKGROUND if the OBJECT is through moving in the
SCENE, thereby saving memory.

SIZE = Adjusts the width and HEIGHT of an OBJECT
changing its size in a specified time.

ANIMSEQN = Sets up the FRAME SEQUENCE for an
animated OBJECT after you type an alphabetic
string (up to 40 characters) into the SEQUENCE
gadget in the ANIMATE SEQUENCE requester.

ANIMCYCLE = Moves through an animation sequence as
fast as possible during the time set.

77

While in the APPEAR requester you may position the OBJECT by dragging it to the desired location by depressing the left mouse button and moving the mouse with the cursor on the OBJECT. The "ghost bar" may be moved for fast positioning in the window. To return from the screen image, click the FRONT-TO-BACK gadget. Click OK to get back to the SCENE window. Position the APPEAR box at the time location you desire.

To MOVE your OBJECT you must drag down a new EFFECTS box and put it on your SCENE track. When asked what kind of EFFECT, pick MOVE TO. This requester will let you select the location of the OBJECT after it moves. You can also make it disappear.

Time is adjusted with the placement of the EFFECTS box and the setting of the ON/OFF ARROWS.

To see this SCENE, select PLAY SCENE from the PROJECT menu.

If you wish to add sound you will have to add a new TRACK in the SCENE SCRIPT. Open the SOUND requester. Stored sounds available for your selection will be presented. Select your pre-recorded SOUND. When loaded, the NAME of the SOUND will be displayed in the IN VIDEO window. Click on the LOUDSPEAKER icon to hear the SOUND. Click the SELECT box to include the SOUND TRACK in your video. A new requester will open asking you what kind of EFFECT you would like to create with SOUND. You may select FETCH or PLAY. If you select FETCH the sound will be preloaded. If you select PLAY, a PLAY EFFECT requester will open. It allows adjusting the RATE, VOLUME and DIRECTION of the SOUND. Click the LOUDSPEAKER icon to sample the SOUND. A click of the left mouse button on OK returns to the SCENE SCRIPT. Now, position the SOUND EFFECT and set the ON/OFF arrows for the duration of the SOUND. For a continuous, uninterrupted SOUND EFFECT you will need to COPY the entire SOUND TRACK by clicking on the TRACK box and then select COPY from the EDIT menu. PASTE this COPY below the original SOUND TRACK by selecting PASTE from the EDIT menu. A ghost of the SOUND TRACK will appear. Move the pointer below the original SOUND TRACK and click the left mouse button to PASTE the COPY. Move the entire box by dragging it with its DRAG BAR to the right about one second in time. This will smooth out the "looping" of the SOUND EFFECT.

Titles and text may be included in your video. Pull down a new EFFECTS box on the VIDEO TRACK. This will become a SCENE EFFECT. Open this SCENE EFFECT by double-clicking the left mouse button on it and a script window for the scene will open. Pull down a new track and pick POLYGON TEXT from the requester. A POLYGON TEXT requester will open. Click the left mouse button on the TEXT bar and type in your TITLE. POLYGON TEXT comes in only one font style but the color, texture and shadow may all be altered. Click the left mouse button on the OK box to return to the SCENE SCRIPT. Bring down a new EFFECT box and select APPEAR. This will allow you to position the TITLE on the screen. A click of the left mouse button on the CENTER box will automatically CENTER the TITLE. Click the left mouse button on the OK box to return to the SCENE window where you can set the time for the TITLE to appear. You can use the MOVE TO command, just as in OBJECTS, to MOVE the TITLE over the screen. POLYGON TEXT may also be rotated and the size may be changed. In addition to the TEXT, there are 26 POLYGON shapes (arrows, triangles, star, boxes and others) that may be animated in the same fashion as POLYGON TEXT.

TEXT LINE however, cannot be rotated nor sized. It offers the advantage of using different font styles.

SCENE SCRIPTS can be named and saved to DISK. To do this, select SAVE AS... from the PROJECT menu and click the left mouse button on the FILE gadget in the SAVE requester. Next, type the NAME of your video and click the left mouse button on SAVE.

You are able to combine pictures produced by an IFF format paint program with the FRAMER utility on the PARTS DISK to generate cel animation. The DELUXE VIDEO CONSTRUCTION SET does not do "tweening" like AEGIS ANIMATOR. Cel animation is like a "flip book" animation where a number of pages have a slightly different version of an OBJECT on each page so that when you flip the pages, an illusion of motion occurs. Each page is a cel. You use the computer paint program to draw the pictures for the cels. For example, if you are using DELUXEPAINT, at the CLI prompt type: (dpaint lo 3) which will let you work in LO-RES and with 8 colors. The DELUXE VIDEO CONSTRUCTION SET is limited to 8 colors so this will insure that your picture will LOAD with the same palette.

For smooth animation, the parts of OBJECTS that are not to appear in motion must be in perfect alignment and the parts that MOVE should relate as well. This is accomplished by constructing a rectangle around the picture image to be animated using a one-pixel brush point. This borders the first cel. Next, capture this picture image, plus the rectangular border as a BRUSH, and deposit it right next to the first rectangle so that the border lines just touch. DO NOT overlap the border lines. Where they meet should form a new border that is two pixels wide. Thus, an identical image is made for the second cel. In this second cel you can make the necessary modifications of the image to give the simulation of movement by erasing and adding to the image. Repeat this cloning, pasting and editing as needed for your animation sequence. SAVE this in the PICTURE drawer of your PARTS storage DISK.

The FRAMER utility will take all these versions of the image which you stored in a drawer and overlap them for showing in an animation sequence.

Put your PARTS DISK in the computer drive and click the left mouse button twice to open PARTS. Click twice on the FRAMER tool icon to open the FRAMER: PICTURE SCREEN. It displays six boxes labelled a-f which represent the cels in sequence. The a = the first cel, b = the second, c = the third and so forth. This FRAME SEQUENCE may be moved around the screen to reposition it over the image by placing the mouse pointer in the DRAG BAR at the top of the "a" box and while the left mouse button is depressed, movement of the mouse will MOVE the boxes. At the bottom of the "a" box on the right corner is a size control gadget. This reduces or enlarges the boxes. Put the mouse pointer inside this size gadget and while the left mouse button is depressed, movement of the mouse will size the boxes. You will need these commands to overlay this FRAME SEQUENCE on top of your bordered images of the animation cels.

You are not limited to the DEFAULT six boxes. If you select CHANGE FRAME from the PROJECT menu in this window you can click the left mouse button on the PLUS (+) or MINUS (-) box at the top of the requester to add or subtract boxes. Pick OK to use or CANCEL to exit without change.

FRAME SEQUENCE normally is from left to right. Click the left mouse button on the DOWN box and on OK to change the sequence from ACROSS to DOWN causing a top to bottom sequence. The number of box columns is set in the ACROSS section and the number of box rows is set in the DOWN section. Click the left mouse button on the PLUS or MINUS box to make any alterations.

Now, select LOAD from the PICTURE menu of FRAMER to LOAD your image by clicking on its NAME with the left mouse button. When your image loads it will be under the FRAME SEQUENCE boxes. Pick CHANGE FRAME from the PROJECT menu to adjust the "a" box so that its upper left corner is covering the upper left corner of the rectangle bordering your image. Use the SIZE box to place the bottom right corners of the "a" box and the rectangle bordering your image. All box and border lines must be congruent. Once the "a" box and cel number one are aligned all the other boxes and cels will be also. Select MAKE OBJECT FROM FRAME with the right mouse button from the PROJECT menu. Select ANIMATE with the right mouse button from the PROJECT menu to see the animation sequence. Place the mouse pointer inside the FRAME and depress the left mouse button while dragging the image to its APPEAR location. This is the screen position where the image will be when you invoke the APPEAR EFFECT. Next, select SAVE with the right mouse button from the OBJECT menu. Type a NAME for your animation and click the left mouse button on SAVE to place your work in DISK storage.

If you LOAD a PICTURE with more than 8 colors a system request will offer to change to the BEST palette of 8 colors or you can pick the CURRENT palette of 8 colors in the video.

To show a video, select OPEN from the PROJECT menu and click the left mouse button on the NAME of the video. Use the PLAYER DISK to show the video. Be sure that the PLAYER drawers have the instruments for MUSIC and the parts for any animation or OBJECT required for your video.

The DELUXE VIDEO CONSTRUCTION SET employs a logical outline structure. These layers are presented on the next pages. While making a video, requesters will give you the options for the EFFECT. Experiment to explore the possibilities of using these techniques and combine them for numerous special EFFECTS. The PLAYER DISK has some demonstration videos on it. Run

81

these and look at their VIDEO SCRIPTS, taking apart each SCENE and studying every EFFECT. This will help you familiarize yourself with the program and the opportunities available to you for the creation of animated videos.

I. VIDEO SCRIPT
   A. VIDEO TRACK
      1. SCENE SCRIPT
         a. SOUND TRACK
            i. FETCH
           ii. PLAY
         b. CONTROL TRACK
            i. CHAIN
           ii. KEYWAIT
           iii. KEYCHAIN
         c. BACKGROUND TRACK
            i. CLEAR
           ii. WIPE
           iii. COLORS
           iv. LOCKCLRS
           v. SIZE
           vi. CUT
           vii. CYCLECLR
           viii. FADE IN
           ix. FADE OUT
           x. PATTERN
         d. FOREGROUND TRACK
           i. DISAPP
           ii. COLORS
           iii. STAMP
           iv. STROBE
           v. LOCKCLRS
           vi. CYCLECLR
           vii. FADE OUT
         e. TEXT LINE TRACK
           i. APPEAR
           ii. DISAPP
           iii. MOVE TO
           iv. STAMP
         f. OBJECT TRACK
           i. FETCH
           ii. APPEAR
           iii. DISAPP
           iv. MOVE TO
           v. STAMP
           vi. SIZE
           vii. ANIMSEQN
           viii. ANIMCYCL

  This introduction will get you started in video. In time you will be producing professional results.

The design of the PALETTE.

CHAPTER TWELVE

USING PAINT AND PRINT PALETTES:

A color printer will not print colors exactly as displayed on a MONITOR screen. This chapter will present a method for creating a working palette and a print palette which will print the colors as shown on the MONITOR. Follow these directions to make a color wheel of a working palette which I call PAINT PALETTE. It displays a primary red, yellow and blue along with the secondary colors of orange, green and violet. In addition, intermediate hues such as yellow-green, blue-green, blue-violet, red-violet, red-orange and yellow-orange are placed on the circle. Other intermediate hues like yellow-yellow-green and yellow-green-green complete the wheel of twenty-four hues. A PAINT PALETTE is created and saved on DISK so it can be loaded and used in paint programs such as DELUXEPAINT. A second palette is made which does not look like the PAINT PALETTE on the MONITOR but when printed on the Okidata Okimate 20 color printer will print a color wheel that looks like the color wheel shown on the MONITOR screen. When you wish to make a print that will have a close resemblance to the colors on the MONITOR, you simply LOAD the PRINT PALETTE so that you are using this palette when you give the PRINT command.

Here is the procedure step by step:

(1) Insert the KICKSTART DISK.

(2) Remove the KICKSTART DISK and insert the DELUXEPAINT DISK and LOAD the DELUXEPAINT program in low-resolution mode.

(3) Using DELUXEPAINT by Electronic Arts, change the screen color to white by clicking the right mouse button after placing the pointer on the white square in the menu. Now place the pointer at CLR on the menu and click on this command to create the white screen.

(4) Select the large round brush by clicking the right mouse button over its symbol on the upper right of the menu. Make the brush large enough to form a large black circle about 1/2 inch thick.

(5) Select black by clicking on the black square of the menu with your left mouse button.

(6) Select OPEN CIRCLE from the menu using the left mouse button and draw a large black circle almost filling the screen.

(7) Select SYMMETRY from the menu with the right mouse button and change the number from 6 to 24 by deleting 6 and typing 24 in the window.

(8) Select SYMMETRY with the left mouse button and choose the ROUND BRUSH symbol with the right mouse button so that you can make a round shape for the hues big enough to fit inside your black circle. By using the 24 SYMMETRY command you can place 24 round shapes inside the circle band. Use white to paint these circles which will be filled with the twenty-four hues we create.

(9) Open the PALETTE by typing a lower case (p) or use the mouse by selecting COLOR CONTROL and PALETTE from the pull-down menu.

(10) Use the sliders to CALIBRATE the Red, Green and Blue mixtures for each of the thirty-two squares beginning with black at the top left as listed on the next page:

PAINT PALETTE

```
00) R0/G0/B0          Black
01) R15/G15/B15       White
02) R2/G2/B2          Very Dark Gray
03) R4/G4/B4          Dark Gray
04) R6/G6/B6          Middle Dark Gray
05) R8/G8/B8          Middle Gray
06) R10/G10/B10       Light Gray
07) R12/G12/B12       Very Light Gray
08) R14/G0/B6         Red
09) R15/G0/B4         Red-Red-Orange
10) R15/G0/B2         Red-Orange
11) R15/G2/B0         Red-Orange-Orange
12) R15/G3/B0         Orange
13) R15/G6/B0         Yellow-Orange-Orange
14) R15/G9/B0         Yellow-Orange
15) R15/G11/B0        Yellow-Yellow-Orange
16) R15/G15/B0        Yellow
17) R8/G11/B0         Yellow-Yellow-Green
18) R3/G6/B0          Yellow-Green
19) R3/G5/B2          Yellow-Green-Green
20) R0/G4/B3          Green
21) R0/G8/B6          Blue-Green-Green
22) R0/G5/B6          Blue-Green
23) R0/G4/B6          Blue-Blue-Green
24) R0/G1/B9          Blue
25) R1/G0/B8          Blue-Blue-Violet
26) R3/G0/B6          Blue-Violet
27) R4/G0/B5          Blue-Violet-Violet
28) R4/G0/B4          Violet
29) R6/G0/B6          Red-Violet-Violet
30) R8/G0/B6          Red-Violet
31) R13/G0/B6         Red-Red-Violet
```

(11) Select PAINTCAN AREA FILL from the menu and
click the left mouse button on yellow and use
the FILL command to fill the top circle with
yellow (16) Fill each circle in turn clockwise
so it follows:

(17),(18),(19),(20),(21),(22),(23),(24),(25),(26),(27),
(28),(29),(30),(31),(32),(9),(10),(11),(12),(13),(14)
and (15) to complete the circle.

(12) Select the STRAIGHT LINE command and black
color and draw lines to connect opposite
circles.

(13) Use the PAINTCAN AREA FILL command to fill the pie wedges with (7),(6),(5),(4),(3) and (2) opposite each other beginning with the wedge to the right of yellow proceeding clockwise to violet. At violet repeat (7),(6),(5),(4),(3) and (2) to complete the gray wedges.

(14) Draw a FILLED CIRCLE with black about two inches in diameter on the screen in the middle of the wheel.

(15) Select FONTS and letter PAINT in white in the middle of the hub.

(16) Save this on DISK and NAME it PAINT PALETTE.

(17) Click on (p) to bring the PALETTE on screen or use the mouse by selecting COLOR CONTROL and PALETTE from the pull-down menu. Use the sliders to create this new palette which follows on the next page:

PRINT PALETTE

```
00) R0/G0/B0            Black
01) R15/G15/B15         White
02) R2/G2/B2            Very Dark Gray
03) R4/G4/B4            Dark Gray
04) R6/G6/B6            Middle Dark Gray
05) R8/G8/B8            Middle Gray
06) R10/G10/B10         Light Gray
07) R12/G12/B12         Very Light Gray
08) R15/G0/B8           Red
09) R15/G0/B5           Red-Red-Orange
10) R15/G0/B2           Red-Orange
11) R15/G0/B0           Red-Orange-Orange
12) R15/G3/B0           Orange
13) R15/G6/B0           Yellow-Orange-Orange
14) R15/G9/B0           Yellow-Orange
15) R15/G12/B0          Yellow-Yellow-Orange
16) R15/G15/B0          Yellow
17) R8/G12/B0           Yellow-Yellow-Green
18) R6/G10/B0           Yellow-Green
19) R3/G10/B0           Yellow-Green-Green
20) R0/G8/B0            Green
21) R0/G10/B4           Blue-Green-Green
22) R0/G11/B8           Blue-Green
23) R0/G12/B13          Blue-Blue-Green
24) R0/G8/B15           Blue
25) R0/G6/B15           Blue-Blue-Violet
26) R0/G4/B15           Blue-Violet
27) R0/G2/B15           Blue-Violet-Violet
28) R0/G0/B15           Violet
29) R5/G0/B15           Red-Violet-Violet
30) R8/G0/B15           Red-Violet
31) R15/G0/B14          Red-Red-Violet
```

(18)   NAME this palette PRINT PALETTE and save it to DISK.

(19) Now you can paint your picture by loading PAINT PALETTE. Clear the screen by clicking CLR on the menu.

(20) Use this PAINT PALETTE to paint your picture.

(21) Save your picture to DISK.

(22) Select SWAP SCREEN from the menu or type a lower case (j).

(23) LOAD the PRINT PALETTE.

(24) Type a lower case (j) to bring your picture up to the front screen.

(25) Select PRINT from the pull down menu to print your picture on the Okidata Okimate 20 Printer.

The image on the screen will change to the hues of this PRINT PALETTE but the print will resemble the picture you created with the PAINT PALETTE.

CHAPTER THIRTEEN

USING COMPUTER TECHNOLOGY WITH OLDER TECHNIQUES

As you progressed through the programs in this book you probably came to the realization that in the creation and development stages of computer art, animation and video the AMIGA is a powerful tool. Studio setup occurs in a few seconds and is seldom slower than a couple of minutes while you boot the system and load a software program thus saving valuable time for work. It allows you to make changes rapidly and easily. The opportunity to save your work at any stage of its development frees you to explore all the possible creative choices thereby unlocking the potential of your image. Changes of color and design may be accomplished in moments and the original or any stage of the design that has been saved to DISK may be recalled letting you branch off from that stage. This is a new level of freedom in the creative process.

Computer graphics do not have to mimic traditional art media, but created images can be reproduced in the traditional art materials to provide a permanent print on 100% rag (acid-free for permanence) paper.

A positive color film transparancy can be made by copying the image from the MONITOR screen. This procedure involves placing a camera on a tripod so that the center of the lens is lined up with the center of the screen. A fast film should be used, like Kodak's Tri-X for black and white or Ektachrome 200 for color slides.

The image, formed on the screen, is made by a moving electron beam that scans the picture in two sections. It takes about one thirtieth of a second to complete an image on the screen, so camera shutter speeds faster than one thirtieth of a second will often cause a dark band across the picture copy. One should use shutter speeds of one eight or one fifteenth of a second. A single lens reflex camera is a good choice. Use a telephoto lens in the 100 to 200mm range. A 135mm is an excellent lens for this. It can be placed far enough away from the MONITOR to let you work the controls and it does not distort the image as a wider lens does. This helps to keep the lines straight. A viewfinder in a camera usually displays a little less than will appear in a slide. Allow for this by cropping or cutting the image slightly on the edges if you wish to fill the frame of the slide with your picture.

Reflections can pose a problem on the surface of the screen. All room lights must be turned off and windows covered. Adjustable, pyramidal boxes are available, which hood the screen, joining the screen and lens, excluding reflections. These boxes should be used if the lights can not be controlled.

You may use a meter reading from a middle gray screen. Fill a screen with a middle gray using one of the paint programs shape fill option. In any event, a series of exposures should be taken, with one at the suggested f-stop; additional exposures should be made by opening up and closing down the lens diaphragm in one-half stop sequences. If you make a test roll of exposures you should set the monitor controls to their detent positions. Record all information and select the best f-stop for a fixed shutter speed based on the best slide. If you bracket, one of the exposures should record a good image of the picture on the screen. Color negative film may be used but the best and most permanent prints are Cibachrome prints made from slides. Cibachrome color prints use permanent dyes. Black and white film is exposed in the same fashion. If a positive black and white slide is required, use Polaroid's Polapan film.

Enlarged prints of the 35mm slides can be made on a Xerox 6500 Color Copier combined with a slide projector attachment and a plastic dot screen placed on top of the platen. This machine makes a clean, hard-edged copy, capturing detail as small as the characters on a type-written page. Many copy centers have these copiers and some provide mail order service. The 6500 has both color and contrast controls, which allow further fine tuning of a print. This copier uses standard 20-pound bond paper; 100% rag art paper like Rives BFK or Arches may be inserted in the machine by a trained operator. Xerox also makes a special transfer paper that allows a slide to be enlarged and transferred to any paper or to a natural fiber cloth. A simple hand iron, set on the heat setting for linen, can be used to transfer the color toners in the latex-coated transfer paper onto the new base material. Thus, large pictures can be made by combining or overlapping the images from several sheets. The transfer paper should be peeled from the base in a smooth, continuous pull, or a line will occur on the print. Colored pencils, pastels, watercolor or acrylic paint may be added to alter the print at this stage.

Print processes requiring color separation negatives are possible if the color separation nagatives are made from a 35mm slide projected in an enlarger onto Kodak's Super-XX film. Three negatives are made, one each through Wratten Red #29, Green #61 and Blue #47B gelatin filters, which are placed between the slide and the Super-XX sheet film. These separation negatives can be used in the gum bichromate and Kwik-Print color processes, which use transparent, light sensitive emulsions and contact negatives to produce full color prints on art papers.

If Kodak's Autoscreen film is substituted for the Super-XX, one can make photo-silkscreen prints, photo-etchings and photolithographs. The half-tone screen is built into the emulsion of this film. Black and white negatives, taken from the monitor screen, can be used to print different colors in the gum bichromate and Kwik-Print processes. These negatives may also be of service when making traditional silver prints, as well as the non-silver processes like platinum, palladium, kallitype, blue cyanotype and Van Dyke brown prints. All of these prints may also be hand-colored.

Kodak's High Speed Duplicating Film #2575 is suitable for enlarging 35mm negatives to a larger-sized negative for techniques requiring a contact negative of the same size as the final print.

Color printers for computers are not as advanced as the computers. The color is not at all as vibrant as the colors seen on the monitor screen. The paper is lacking in textural interest as well. Presently, the best color is being printed on the Okidata Okimate 20 Color Printer. This inexpensive printer uses a heat transfer from a three color wax ribbon and deposits dots of the three colors from a 24 x 24 pin head. These small dots are mixed by the eye and are capable of some rich and subtle color.

With these techniques, computer graphics can be combined with the traditional media of the artist to create the fine art of the future.

CHAPTER FOURTEEN

GALLERY

95

Steve Freedman #41

97

Christopher Oakes
'87

101

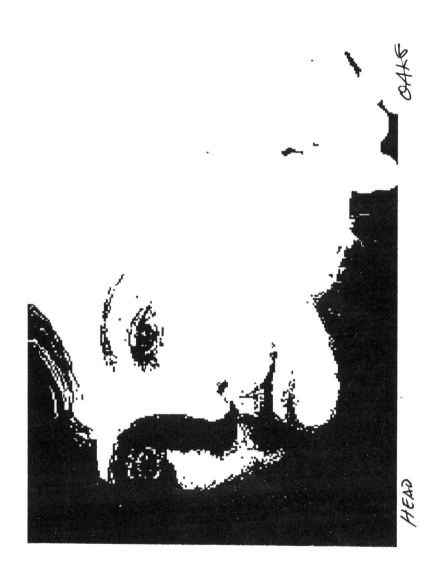

HEAD

OAKS

103

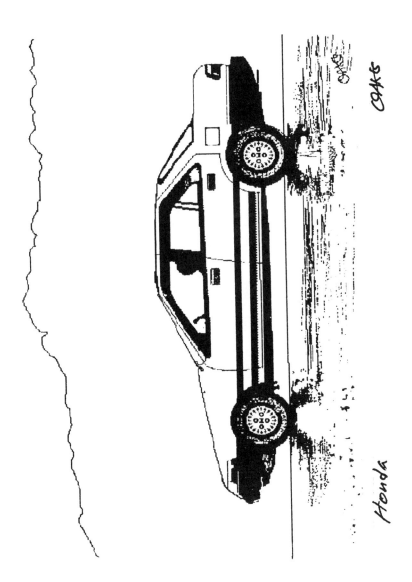

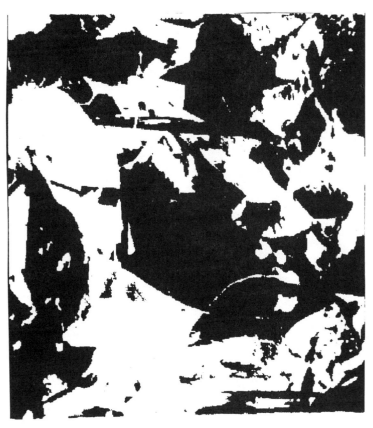

Richard Johnson

107

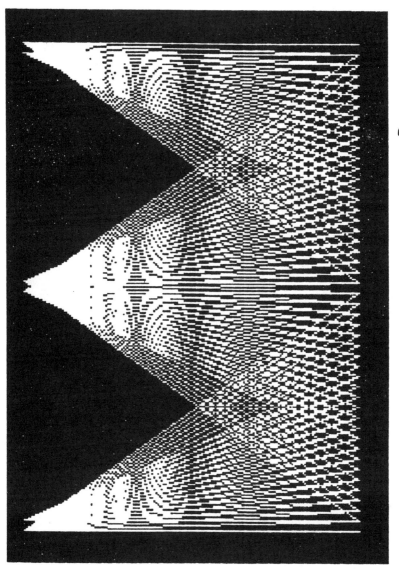

Steve Frautschi #3

109

119

REVERT p. 29
RGB pp. 46, 63, 64, 65, 67
RGB OUT p. 67
ROTATE pp. 13, 14, 59
ROTATE ANY ANGLE p. 13
ROTATE AROUND X p. 57
ROTATE AROUND Y p. 57
ROTATE IN PLANE p. 56
ROTATE TO p. 83

-S-

SATURATION p. 64
SAVE pp. 17, 18, 26, 30, 44, 64, 79, 81
SAVE AS COLORS p. 48
SAVE AS... p. 18
SAVE IFF p. 64
SAVE RGB p. 64
SAVEAS... pp. 18, 38, 39, 79
SCENE pp. 75, 77, 78, 79, 82
SCENE EFFECT p. 79,
SCENE SCRIPT pp. 75, 76, 77, 82
SCREEN FORMAT pp. 23, 25
SCREEN SIZE PAGE p. 25
SCRIPT pp. 55, 69, 70, 71, 73, 75, 76, 77, 78, 79, 82
SCROLL ALL pp. 69, 70
SCROLL UP pp. 69, 70
SEE TWEEN AT BEGIN p. 58
SEE TWEEN AT END p. 58
SEED FILL pp. 49
SELECT pp. 57, 76, 77, 78
SELECT ALL p. 57
SELECT BUTTON p. 1
SELECT POINT p. 57
SELECT POINTS p. 57
SELECT POLYGON p. 57
SELECT SEGMENT p. 57
SEQ PNTS p. 51
SEQUENCE pp. 77, 80, 81
SET DESTINATION p. 43
SET SOURCE p. 43
SHADE pp. 9, 20, 21, 24
SHAPE pp. 32, 41, 42, 43, 45, 49, 52
SHAPE OPTIONS pp. 42, 49, 50, 51, 52, 54
SHAPE OPTIONS MENU pp. 42, 49, 52
SHAPE OPTIONS OFF pp. 42
SHAPE OPTIONS ON p. 42
SHARE 1 pp. 49, 50, 51, 52
SHARE 2 pp. 51, 52
SHARPNESS pp. 64, 65
SHEAR pp. 13, 14
SHIFT KEY pp. 12, 13

ABOUT THE AUTHOR

John Warren Oakes oversees the Electronic Art Lab at Western Kentucky University where he is Professor of Art. He is the author of MINIMAL APERTURE PHOTOGRAPHY USING PINHOLE CAMERAS and has written about computer graphics for *AmigaWorld* magazine. His work has been exhibited in regional, national and international exhibitions.